FOOD AND BEVERAGE MANAGEMENT

FOOD AND BEVERAGE MANAGEMENT

PIYUSH BHATNAGAR
NITIN POPLI

2007

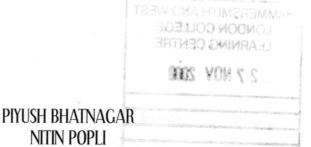

SBS Publishers & Distributors Pvt. Ltd.
New Delhi

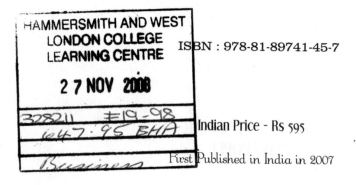

ISBN : 978-81-89741-45-7

Indian Price - Rs 595

First Published in India in 2007

© Reserved

Published by:
SBS PUBLISHERS & DISTRIBUTORS PVT. LTD.
2/9, Ground Floor, Ansari Road, Darya Ganj,
New Delhi - 110002, INDIA
Tel: 23289119, 41563911
Email: mail@sbspublishers.com
www.sbspublishers.com

Printed at Chaman Enterprises, New Delhi.

Preface

This book has been written to explain the complexities of managing food and beverage outlets. The purpose is to examine the wide range of subject areas that come within the orbit of operational food and beverage management. It covers various areas such as food and beverage production, quality control, and financial aspects in food and beverage management.

An attempt is made in this book to introduce to the readers the important aspects of food and beverage management. Authors do not claim any original contribution in this book, standard publications and other works that are duly acknowledged.

We owe a debt of gratitude to a large number of friends and well-wishers. Our special thanks to our parents and our teachers and who constantly encourage us during this work. The opinions expressed in this book are entirely ours and we take the responsibility for any short-comings, if any. We express our sincere thanks to our publishers, SBS Publishers & Distributors, New Delhi and their efficient editorial staff who helped in publishing this book.

Mr. Piyush Bhatnagar
Mr. Nitin Popli

v

Contents

One

Food and Beverage Management

Introduction

The provision of food and beverages away from home forms a substantial part of the activities of the hotel and catering industry. Like the industry of which it is a part, food and beverage operations are characterized by their diversity. Outlets include private and public sector establishments and range from small privately owned concerns to large international organizations and from prison catering to catering in the most luxurious hotels.

If the hotel and catering industry is considered to cover all undertakings concerned with the provision of food, drink and accommodation away from home, this will naturally include all food and beverage outlets. In other words, food and beverage provision is simply one element of a broader hotel and catering industry. In conceptual terms, this raises few problems except possibly with take-away food establishments where in some cases the food may be taken home for consumption even though it is prepared and provided away from home. In practice, however, there are a number of difficulties in considering the hotel and catering industry as embracing all food and beverage establishments and outlets. This arises because, following a number of official attempts at definition, the hotel and catering industry is often considered to have a much narrower scope. The official definitions exclude many food and beverage outlets. For example the Standard Industrial Classification (CSO 1980) gives hotel and catering a reasonably broad coverage but even here parts of employee and welfare catering are either omitted or included in other sectors. This book adopts the broadest possible approach aiming to consider all types of food and beverage operation wherever they may appear.

Standard Industrial Classification

For analytical purposes, economically similar activities may be grouped together into industries, for example into agriculture, motor vehicle manufacture, retail distribution, catering, and national government service. A system used to group activities in this way is described as and industrial classification. Such a classification usually starts with a small number of broad groups of activities that are then subdivided into progressively narrower groups so that the classification can be used with varying amounts of detail for different purposes.

The Standard Industrial Classification provides a detailed and reliable classification of businesses into groups but, as described earlier, does not give a totally comprehensive picture of the activities of the hotel and catering industry, classification provides a consistent format for the interpretation of government statistics but it does not help to understand the complexity of food and beverage operations and their characteristics.

Size and Scope of Food and Beverage Operations

The statistics that are available from different sources on the size and scope of food and beverage operations do not give a consistent picture because of the different bases used for their collection. Market power makes a clear distinction between those operations run for profit and those operations run at cost. Their categories are simple and straightforward but the 'leisure' category needs a little explanation. This category includes catering provision in historic properties, gardens, museums, zoos, theme parks, cinemas, theatres, leisure centers and sports centers, clubs and events.

Looking at the number of outlets in each of the sectors, hotels have the largest and pubs have the second largest number of outlets operating for profit. The leisure sector is the third largest and is growing in importance. Cafes and take-away are the fourth largest but are reducing in size, perhaps to be replaced by a growing number of fast food operations still a relatively small number overall. Restaurants remain reasonably static in fifth place, while the smallest sector (travel related catering) is also static. On the cost side, education has the largest number of outlets but has dropped slightly over the four years, as has the staff-catering sector, which falls into third place behind the growing numbers in the health care sector. The services sector is relatively small but has grown slightly. Overall the profit side has almost three times the number of outlets than the cost side.

Looking at the number of meals served, on the profit side, pubs are by far the largest sector and have increased rapidly over the four years despite the reduction in the number of outlets. The cafes/take-away and leisure sectors serve about the same number of meals but while the numbers of meals served in leisure is on the increase, the number served in cafes/take-away is declining. Despite being the largest sector in terms of number of outlets, hotels are only fourth in the number of meals served although this would appear to be increasing. Staff caters serves the most meals on the cost side of the industry but there is some evidence that this is declining slightly. The second largest sector is education, which is also declining, followed by health care, which is also declining slightly, perhaps as day surgery and short stays become more common. The smallest number of meals is served to the services and this too is declining. Overall the profit side serves almost twice as many meals as the cost sector and continues to grow reasonably strongly while the cost side seems to be on a slight downward trend.

Classification of Food and Beverage Operations

It is possible to make a number of distinctions between the many different types of food and beverage outlets. First, there is a distinction between those outlets that operate on a strictly commercial basis and those that are subsidize. A second distinction concerns the type of market served. In some cases, the market is confined to restricted groups, as for example in a hospital or prison, while in other cases the outlet is open to the public at large. A third distinction is between outlets where catering is the main activity of the undertaking, as for example in a privately owned commercial restaurant, and those where it is a secondary activity, as is the case with travel catering or school meal catering. A final distinction appears between outlets that are in public ownership and those in private ownership. To a certain extent there is a rough compatibility between the distinctions. On the one hand, captive markets tend to be in public ownership and to be a subsidiary activity of the undertaking. On the other hand, the commercial outlets tend to be in the private sector, to serve the general public and to be the main activity of the undertaking. In brief, the subsidized sector is not normally available to the public at large and normally provides catering only as an activity that is both secondary to the main business and available only to restricted groups. These broad divisions however do not hold true in all cases.

In deed the exceptions are numerous and beyond the broad categories they tend to devalue any generalizations.

Using some of the above distinctions, it is possible to classify food and beverage outlets into a number of broad sectors. Figure illustrates one way of breaking down the industry into sectors. The figure shows a distinction between purely commercial operations and those, which accrue subsidies in some way. The purely commercial operations may be in public or private ownership and include outlets where catering is the main activity as well as those where it is a secondary activity, as for example catering in theatres or shops. In the case of the commercial sector, a secondary division is shown between outlets that have a restricted market and those, which are open to the general, public. The subsidized operations similarly may be in public or private ownership. A distinction is drawn between catering in institutions where public ownership dominates and catering for employees where private ownership is also of importance. Almost by definition subsidized catering tends to be available only to restricted markets. As with any classification, there are of course areas of overlap. There are two of particular importances here. The first overlap concern catering in various private schools, colleges and hospitals, and in some offices and works canteens where the catering is not in any way subsidized but run on strictly commercial lines. These outlets appear under the heading of the commercial sector as commercial catering for a restricted market as shown in figure. The second issue concerns the many subsidized or welfare catering outlets that are operated by catering contractors who are they strictly organized on commercial lines. These have not been separated in figure because although the operators themselves may be commercial companies, this does not affect the fact that the end product is normally subsidized for the market.

There are two reasons for using this classification here. First, it provides a very broad coverage of food and beverage outlets broader, for example, than many of the official definitions and classifications of the hotel and catering industry. The second reason for using this classification is that it is based on distinctions that

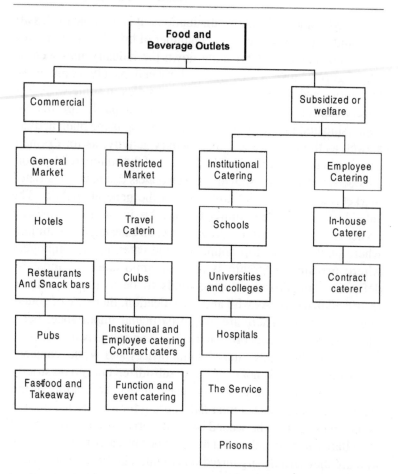

have a significant bearing upon most aspects of the operation of the catering activity. For example the difference between subsidized catering and commercial catering not only embraces differences of objectives but also covers differences in markets served, differences in organizations involved and differences in marketing and business strategy using this classification, the aim here is to outline the different types of food and beverage outlets and to identify their main characteristics. This then serves as a basis for a consideration of issues of relevance to food and beverage operations in general.

Commercial Sector

Commercial food and beverage outlets may be defined as those operations in which profit is a primary concern. Such outlets exist not only in private ownership but also in the publicly owned sector of the economy where, for example, a local leisure center may seek to operate catering outlets on commercial lines. Also, it is worth noting that in the commercial sector, catering may be the main activity of the organization or it may be a secondary or additional service to customers as, for example, catering in department stores or theatres. A broad distinction can be made between catering for a restricted market and catering for a general market. In the case of the former, the market can be restricted in a number of ways, by way of membership criteria as in the case of catering in clubs or by the fact that the catering is only available to those engaged in a specific activity as in the case of travel catering or employee catering. However, there will be some overlap in some cases. For example, catering at a railway station, bus or airport terminal is normally open to the traveler as well as to the general public, while catering on the train, bus or plane itself is limited to those traveling.

Commercial Catering for General Market

Hotels

The provision of food and beverage facilities in hotels ranges from a self-service style often used for breakfast service to full silver service used at the luxury end of the market. In resort hotels, the food and beverage facilities are often presented as one of the more important features of the hotel because the guests may be staying at the hotel for some time rather than just a night

7

or so as may be the case in transient hotels. The types of food and beverage outlets found in hotels include silver service restaurants, licensed bars, coffee shops and snack bars, carvery and buffet restaurants, gueridon service and banqueting facilities. Some of these facilities are only available to hotel residents, or 'in-house trade', for example room service; while the hotel to attract outside custom advertises the others, for example coffee shops and other restaurants, externally.

Restaurants and Snack Bars

The primary function of commercial restaurants is the provision of food and beverages. As these restaurants do not have any in house trade, they depend on their location and the volume of passing trade and the reputation they develop from word of mouth advertising. The various types of restaurants include snack bars, cafes, and coffee shops; take away, theme restaurants, ethnic restaurants, haute cuisine restaurants, etc. These diverse types of restaurant have an equally wide range of service styles, ranging from the self service cafeterias through to the more elaborate methods of table service found in luxury restaurants, and those particular service techniques specific to specialty restaurants such as Chinese, Polynesian, Indian and Japanese. A separate bar area may be provided for before or after meal drinks, providing the double advantage of offering the customer a place to sit and relax away from the dining area and allowing a faster seat turnover in the restaurant.

Public Houses

Public houses consist of a varied group of establishments, which mainly offer the general public alcoholic liquor for sale for consumption on and off the premises. The supply of food, at one time ancillary to liquor, is an increasingly dominant element in the 'product mix' for the consumer. The characteristics of public houses are, first, that they require a magistrate's license to operate that is only granted to suitable persons and, second, that many public houses are owned by a brewery company, providing an integration of their production with the retail distribution of alcoholic beverages.

To become more competitive and to meet customer's demands, the catering premises in most pubs have improved considerably in recent years. Some brewery companies have classified their public houses by the level of catering offered. This ranges from those offering only sandwiches through to hot and cold snacks, a cold buffet counter, a bistro type operation, a griddle or steak bar and a full a la carte menu. The range of food items offered is mainly of the convenience food type but at times extends to the total fresh food items. Several brewery companies market specific pubs by the type of catering offered with a brand image.

Fast Food and Take-away

This sector of the industry is concerned with the preparation and service of food and beverages quickly for immediate sale to the customer for consumption either on or off the premises. These range from the traditional fish and chip shop through a series of ethnic cuisines to the high street branded operations.

At the fast food end of the market, there are a number of characteristics common to many of the outlets. First, units are usually themed around a product (for example, hamburgers) a range of products (for example, fish or pizza), or products of a country (for example, Chinese, Italian). This 'product' is very well marketed, for example from a themed product to decor and atmosphere, to the high and consistent standard of the product, to advertising on television, local radio and newspapers, to the container boxes for take-away items. Second, the method of food production is often partially or fully automated; often-using commodities of the convenience type (for example, frozen chips, concentrated beverage syrups), there by deskilling the job and restricting the product range variable. Similarly, the method of food service is simplified and basic. Third, the pricing of the items and the ASP per customer lie within a fairly distinct known price band. Finally, the units are often owned by large chains or are franchised.

Commercial Catering for Restricted Market

Travel Catering

Travel catering i.e. road, rail, air and sea, has a number of characteristics not commonly associated with other food and beverage outlets. It frequently involves the feeding of a large number of customers arriving together at a catering facility, and who need to be catered for in a specific time, for example, on board a plane. The plane only carries sufficient food and beverage supplies for a specific number of meal periods. If for any reason this food cannot be served to customers, alternative supplies may not be readily available. The service of the food and beverages may be particularly difficult due to the physical conditions within the service area, for example, turbulence on board a plane. The types of restaurants described previously are usually catering for a specific and identifiable socio economic market. Travel catering often has to cater for 'mixed markets'. Finally, there are the problems of staffing these food and beverage facilities: the extra costs involved in the transportation and service of the food and beverages; space restrictions and the problem of security while the operation is in transit.

Four main types of travel catering may be identified:

Road Catering

Road catering has progressed from the inns and taverns of earlier days used by those traveling on foot and horseback to the present-day motorway service areas and other roadside catering outlets. These service areas are often open twenty four hours a day and have a particular problem of staffing as some employees have to be brought to and from work over a distance of twenty to thirty miles. Also, because of their isolated locations, the hours they are open and the sheer volume of numbers involved at peak periods, these service areas are also particularly prone to vandalism and littering. They do, however, provide a valuable catering service to the traveling public and their food and beverage facilities usually include self-service and waiter service restaurants, vending machines and take-away foods and beverages. High street fast food operations are also now appearing both on motorway service areas and as freestanding drive-through

Rail Catering

Rail catering may be conveniently divided into two areas, terminal catering and in-transit catering. Catering at railway terminals usually comprises licensed bars, self-service and waiter service restaurants, fast food and take-away units, supplemented by vending machines dispensing hot and cold foods and beverages. In transit catering can feature three kinds of service. The first is the traditional restaurant car service where breakfast, lunch and dinner are organized in sittings and passengers go to the restaurant car for service where appropriate seating accommodation is provided, and then return to their seats on the train after their meal. In a Pullman service, these meals are delivered direct to the seat of first class passengers only. The second type of service is the buffet car, which is a self-service operation in which passengers go to the car and buy light refreshments over the counter. The third is a trolley service where snacks and drinks are delivered to customers at their seats.

Airline Catering

Airline catering has increased and developed considerably over the past twenty-five years. Originally consisting of sandwiches and flasks of tea, coffee and alcoholic beverages, the progress to today's full and varied service has paralleled that of aircraft development itself. Like the railways, airline catering falls into two main areas terminal catering, and 'in-transit' or 'in-flight' catering. Food and beverage outlets at air terminals usually consist of self-service and waiter service restaurants, supplemented by vending machines and licensed bars. The in-flight catering service varies considerably with the class of travel, type and duration of flight. For the economy travelers, the food and beverage portions are highly standardized with the meals portioned into plastic trays that are presented to the passengers and from which they eat their meals. Disposable cutlery, napkins, etc. may be used to increase the standard of hygiene and reduce the weight carried and storage space required. For first class travelers there is virtually no portion control. Service is from a gueridon trolley, where food is portioned in front of the customers and any garnishes, sauces, etc. are added according to their immediate requirements. The crockery used may be bone china and this combines with fine glassware and cutlery to create an atmosphere of high-class dining. A characteristic of airline catering is that this service is often contracted out to a specialist-catering firm, which will supply a similar service to many airlines. The meal is usually included in the price of the fare and a particular feature is now made of cabin service facilities by different airlines. The growth in air travel has made competition fierce, and the area of food service is now a particularly competitive aspect of the total service offered by an airline.

Sea or Marine Catering

Sea or marine catering varies from the provision of food and beverages on the short sea route ferries to the large cruise or passenger liners where the catering facilities are an important part of the service offered by the shipping line and are usually included in the price of the fare. On the cruise liners the standard of catering facilities is high because they are an important sales feature in a competitive activity. On the short sea routes, however, price is usually a more important factor and because of the necessity to feed large numbers of people in a short time the catering service provided is usually of the popular and fast food type.

Clubs

Clubs, as a sector of the hotel and catering industry, are establishments offering food and drink, occasionally with accommodation, to members and their bona fide guests. The types of clubs range from working men's clubs, to political party clubs, social clubs, sporting clubs, restaurant clubs, to the private exclusive clubs.

Proprietary clubs are licensed clubs, owned by an individual or company and operated by them for profit, and as such require a justice's license to operate. Many such clubs resemble licensed restaurants with a substantial part of their turnover obtained from the sales of food. Another growing sector comprises sports or health clubs that offer their members sporting, fitness and leisure facilities but where food is an auxiliary service.

In registered clubs the management is responsible to an elected committee. The members own all the property including the food and drink, and pay their subscriptions to a common fund. As a non-profit making club that belongs to all the members and provides a service to the members, it does not require a justice's license to operate, simply to be registered. The turnover of members' clubs is mainly obtained from the sale of drinks that are normally sold at a competitive price, as the profit element in clubs is lower than, for example, in public houses.

Institutional and Employee Catering

Institutional and employee catering will be dealt with in detail under the heading of subsidized and welfare catering, as indeed most of these types of operations are run on some form of a subsidized basis. It is worth considering, however, that in parts of the private sector such catering activities may be operated on a commercial basis. For example, in many private hospitals and private schools the catering function is operated very much with commercial objectives in mind. Increasingly, contract caterers are providing catering services to the general public on behalf of their clients, for example in leisure centers, theatres or shops.

Function and Event Catering

Function and event catering may be described as the service of food and beverages at a specific time and place, for a given number of people, to an agreed menu and price. Examples of function catering include social functions, such as weddings and dinner dances, business functions such as conferences, meetings and working lunches and those functions that are organized for both social and business reasons such as out-door catering at a sports event, show or exhibition. Function catering is found in both the commercial and noncommercial sectors of the catering industry. In the commercial sector, function catering could be a specialist organization operating in its own function facilities or an outdoor catering specialist operating in a vast range of clients or rented facilities or within marquees, or as a separate department within a hotel. Anyone who has visited a major sporting event cannot fail to be impressed by the scale and range of catering that takes place within the 'tented village'. Indeed some visitors seem to take more interest in the food and beverage provision than in the sports event they have been invited to attend. In the non-commercial sector, function catering is rarely the primary reason for providing the establishment with catering facilities. Such establishments include hospitals, schools, industrial cafeterias, etc. where the functions are not usually organized on a purely profit basis as they are in the commercial sector, but rather to serve a specific need of the organization.

Subsidized or Welfare Sector

Subsidized or welfare food and beverage establishments may be defined as those operations in which making a profit from the catering facility is not the outlet's primary concern. Since the operations are either completely or partially subsidized by a parent body, such establishments' primary obligation is the well being and care of their customers or patients. Unlike customers frequenting commercial sector operations, these customers often do not have a choice of catering facilities, for example in hospitals and schools. Some non-commercial operations are subsidized by government bodies that dictate an allowance per head, or by parent companies that may have a similar arrangement.

A distinction can be made between institutional catering and employee catering facilities, for example, in hospitals and schools. Non-commercial operations embrace catering in institutions such as prisons, schools and hospitals. An important characteristic of this type of catering is that the market is not only usually restricted to the residents of the institutions but also in most cases it is captive.

In addition, institutional catering may be completely subsidized. Employee catering can be in public or private ownership and covers the provision of food and beverage services to employees. The degree of subsidy in this type of operation varies considerably and in many cases the market is not entirely captive. In other words, the catering outlet may be competing with the catering facilities provided at nearby restaurants, pubs and take-away or with food bought in by the workers from their homes.

Institutional Catering

Institutional catering establishments include schools, universities, colleges, hospitals, the Services, and HM prisons. In some of these establishments no charge is made to certain groups of customers to pay for the provision of the food and beverage services as they are completely or partially subsidized by various government funds. This is the part of the catering industry also referred to as the institutional sector.

Schools

The school meal catering service was formerly is structured on a dietary basis with a daily or weekly per capita allowance to ensure that the children obtained adequate nutritional levels from their meals. Most of the schools used to operate their dining rooms on a family type service or a self-service basis with the traditional meat and two vegetarian lunch being very much the norm. There has been a shift away from this conventional arrangement to the provision of a snack type lunch as an alternative to or replacement for the main meal. Many schools now provide 'snack meals' such as baked potatoes, pizzas, sandwiches, rolls, pies, soups, yogurts, etc., and the children may choose from this selection in a normal cafeteria fashion. Some areas have drastically cut their school meal service and are simply providing dining-room space for the children to bring in their own lunches from home. Whether these trends will continue in the future is debatable. It does seem likely, however, that now introduced, the snack-type meal will remain as an alternative to the traditional school meal. Many local education authorities contract out this service to specialist contract caterers.

Universities and Colleges

All institutions of further and higher education provide some form of catering facilities for the academic, administrative, technical and secretarial staff as well as for full and part time students and visitors. The catering service in this sector of the industry suffers from an under utilization of its facilities during the three vacation periods and in many instances at the weekends. Universities are autonomous bodies and are responsible for their own catering services. University catering units have traditionally been of two basic kinds: residential facilities attached to halls that may serve breakfast and evening meals within an inclusive price per term, and central facilities that are open to all students and staff and usually serve lunches and snacks throughout the day with beverages. These catering facilities have to compete openly with the students' union services and independently staffed senior common rooms.

Residential students pay in advance for their board and lodgings. This method has been abandoned by many universities in recent years that have provided reasonable kitchen facilities in the residences to enable students to prepare and cook their own meals if they wish to. Others have introduced a pay-as-you-eat system for residential students. Unfortunately, this has led to reduce catering revenue from students. Non-residential students are provided with an on-site catering provision that has to compete against all other forms of locally provided catering, with ease of accessibility and some level of subsidy being the main attractions. Increasingly, caterers are turning to ideas from the high street operations to attract and keep their predominantly young adult clientele. To offset the losses incurred and to achieve a position of breakeven in catering, universities have seen the advantages of making their residential and catering facilities available at commercial rates to outside bodies for meetings, conferences and for holidays during the vacation periods.

Hospitals

Hospital catering facilities have improved considerably over the past ten to twenty years with the result that new hospitals in particular are benefiting from well planned and managed catering services. Hospital catering is a specialized form of catering as the patient is normally unable to move elsewhere and choose alternative facilities and therefore special attention must be given to the food and beverages so that encouragement is given to eat the meal provided.

The hospital catering service is normally structured on a per capita allowance for patients but with staff paying for all of their meals. A decentralized approach was used in many hospitals where the patients' food and beverages were portioned at the point of delivery in the wards. This often resulted however, in patients' receiving cold, unappetizing meals because of the time between the food being prepared and the patients actually receiving it. This method of food service is commonly replaced by a centralized approach that involves the preparation of the patient's trays in or close to the main production area. From here trucks or mechanical conveyors to the various floors transport them, and from they're directly to the patients so that there should be little delay between the food being plated and served to the patient. Another trend has seen hospital catering open for tender by contract caterers where in many instances a centralized production system for several nearby hospitals may have to be operated to be viable.

Services

The Services include the armed forces, Navy, Army and Air Force, the police and fire service, and some government departments. The armed forces often have their own specialist catering branches; Civil service organizations such as the Metropolitan Police force also have their own catering departments. The levels of food and beverage facilities within the Services vary from the large self-service cafeterias for the majority of personnel, to high-class traditional restaurants for more senior members of staff. A considerable number of functions are also held by the services leading to both small and large scale banqueting arrangements.

Prisons

Working on a very limited budget, the diet for the inmates is based upon fixed weekly quantities of specific named food commodities with a small weekly cash allowance per head for fresh meat and a further separate weekly cash allowance per head for the local purchase of dietary extras of which a proportion must be spent on fresh fruit. The catering within the prisons is the responsibility of the prison governor with delegated responsibility being given to a catering officer, with much of the actual cooking and service being done by the inmates themselves.

Employee Catering

As already outlined, this is the provision of catering services to employees. The activity may be performed either directly by the employer, or sub contracted out to contract caterers. A direct or in-house catering service that is running smoothly and being well managed is unlikely to change to using a contractor. Those operations, however, that are experiencing difficulty may be wise to consider employing the services of a catering contractor but in doing so must also be sure to define exactly what is required of the contractor in terms of level of service, costs per employee head, revenue, etc. In providing a catering service for their employees, the parent company may decide at one extreme to subsidize the facility or at the other to pass all the costs on to the customer. There are various formulas for subsidizing prices, but a general one is for the revenue from the Catering facility to cover food and labour costs with the remaining costs, such as premises and equipment, fuel costs and management fees to be met by the employer. In some sectors of the industry the catering service may be provided virtually free with the employees making only a small token payment per meal

A variety of catering styles and levels of service is found in industrial catering situations. The majority of the market is catered for by popular and fast food facilities incorporating different methods of service, such as self-service cafeterias, buffet restaurants and vending operations. Management in large companies may also have the additional choice of waiter service facilities. At the top end of the industrial catering market, that is those facilities catering for directors and executives, the standard of food and service can equal or exceed that found in commercial high-class restaurants.

Catering contractors may be employed for a variety of reasons but it is usually because the company sees itself as engaged in a certain field of industry, manufacturing for example, and therefore does not wish to involve itself in catering, or the company is dissatisfied with the existing catering service and seeks a change.

In return for operating a company's catering service, the contract caterers charge a management fee, between 3 and 5 per cent of turnover being the norm. For this fee the contract caterers may install a catering facility if there is not one already there, staff the unit, and then be concerned with its day-to-day operation. Ideally, if the catering operation is being satisfactorily run within the parent company's guidelines, the catering contractors should manage the operation completely, only needing to report to the company at management meetings and other predetermined intervals.

The number of food and beverage outlets reviewed here illustrates the diversity of the hotel and catering industry. It is diverse because it caters for a varied and growing eating out market. As with all marketing situations, it is prone to change, but although there may be shifts from one sector to another in volume terms, within the general structure of the industry the future points the way towards growth and expansion.

Cost and Market Orientation

It is convenient at this point to discuss the broad distinction between cost and market orientation within the hotel and catering industry, as these two terms are closely associated with the particular sectors' of the industry that have been identified. Examples of cost orientation are identified in the industry particularly in the welfare sector such as catering in prisons, for patients in hospitals and often for 'in-house' employee restaurants, while market orientation examples are found in the hotels, restaurants, popular and fast food sectors.

It is arguable that all sectors of the industry would be better to employ a market-oriented approach. A market oriented business displays the following characteristics:

1. A high percentage of fixed costs, for example rent, rates, management salaries, depreciation of buildings and equipment. This high percentage of fixed costs remains fixed regardless of any changes in the volume of sales. A hotel restaurant is an example of an operation with high fixed costs.

2. A greater reliance on increases in revenue rather than decreases in costs to contribute to the profit levels of the establishment. The implication here is that in seeking to increase the business's profitability, more emphasis must be given to increasing sales (for example, by increasing the average spend of the customers or by increasing the number of customers) rather than by reducing costs. For this reason the close monitoring of all sales in a market oriented business becomes of prime importance.

3. An unstable market demand for the product, thereby requiring a greater emphasis on all forms of selling and merchandising of the product to eliminate shortfalls in sales.

4. More likely to have a more flexible pricing policy.

A cost oriented business displays the following characteristics:

(a) A lower percentage of fixed costs, but a higher percentage of variable costs such as food and beverage costs. The percentage of variable costs in cost oriented establishments varies with changes in the volume of the business's sales. Employee restaurants are often found with a lower percentage of fixed costs.

(b) A greater reliance on decreases in costs rather than increases in sales to contribute to the budgeted profit levels of the establishment. Thus in seeking to increase the performance level (budgeted revenue and profit) of a cost oriented business more emphasis should be given to reducing the overall costs of the operation in such areas as purchasing, portion sizes, and labour levels.

(c) A relatively stable market demand for the product. In comparison to market oriented businesses, cost oriented operations enjoy a reasonably stable demand for their products. The potential market for their products is considerably greater, so that operations such as catering outlets in industrial plants, universities and colleges are able to cater to a much wider market.

(d) More likely to have a more traditional fixed pricing policy.

There are those areas of the hotel and catering industry that cannot be precisely defined as either cost or market oriented in that they display characteristics of both orientations at different times during their business. Service industries, such as food and beverage operations, differ from manufacturing in several ways. The customer is present at the time of both production and service. In manufacturing the customer is not present during the production process.

In food and beverage operations, the customer is involved in the creation of the service that is consumed at the point of production with little or no time delay between production and service. The customer is not involved in the creation of manufactured products and there may be a considerable time lag between production and service. Services cannot be examined in advance, they are highly perishable and cannot be stored, all adding to difficulties in the quality control of service products; in manufacturing goods can be made in advance of demand and stored allowing more time for control procedures. Finally, services have a larger intangible element in many of their products than manufactured goods do and for this reason have traditionally been more difficult to quantify and evaluate.

Food and Beverage Management

Definitions of management are numerous with writers using different words and phrases to describe the same activity, but if allowance is made for this there is some broad agreement about managers' functions.

First, they are involved in the planning process setting objectives, making decisions about which direction the organization should take that is, formulating policies.

Second, managers decide how these objectives should be achieved and by whom. This involves analyzing tasks and assigning them to individuals or groups.

Third, managers are involved in staff motivation in such a way as to move the organization through them in the direction formulated at the planning stage, to achieve the stated objectives.

Fourth, managers have a controlling function including the comparison of actual performance to that forecast at the initial planning stage and taking any necessary steps to correct any deviation from agreed objectives. The controlling may be done by observation, by analysis of accounting records and reports or by analysis of recorded statistical data.

These four management functions planning, organizing, motivating and controlling can be translated into the functions of the food and beverage manager. In a food and beverage department, the planning process involves the setting of several basic policies: a financial policy dealing with envisaged profitability or cost constraints of the establishment; a marketing policy defining the market to be catered for and a catering policy defining the main objectives of operating the food and beverage facilities and the methods by which such objectives are to be achieved. Such policies would be decided at a senior level of management. The tasks needed to achieve these objectives would then be assigned to individuals who should receive job descriptions detailing the purpose of their tasks, the responsibilities of the individuals, who they are responsible to, etc. Here food and beverage managers work in conjunction with the personnel department in producing job descriptions and appointing on-the job trainers to help train new staff.

The motivation of the staff of the food and beverage department is an important function of food and beverage managers. This may be undertaken in several ways for example, by helping individuals who are undertaking common tasks to form into groups so that a 'team spirit' may develop, by encouraging staff management committee meetings, or at a more basic level to see that full training is given so that job anxieties are reduced for employees from the beginning.

Finally, there is the element of control in the food and beverage department. This involves the checking of actual performance against, expectations or forecasts, and in the case of any wide deviations, to locate the problem area and rectify it, and to take whatever steps are possible to prevent the problem occurring again. The functions of food and beverage managers in coordinating the food and beverage department are therefore numerous, and it is important that they should use all the tools of management available to them. An organization chart should be produced showing the position of the food and beverage department within the context of the total establishment. An organization chart presents graphically the basic groupings and relationships of positions, and a general picture of the formal organization structure. Using a critical incident methodology, the research collected situations in which managers felt that their contributions or actions had made a significant difference to the outcome of a situation; somewhere the manager's skills and knowledge were used well, and somewhere the respondents felt their skills and knowledge were lacking. These incidents were then categorized into the four key areas of managing operations, managing the business, managing people and personal skills. Each of these areas was then divided into categories. These fifteen categories represent the key areas of skills and knowledge that any manager in the hospitality industry needs in order to be effective.

To allow for the differences in the titles and roles between industrial sectors the following management levels were used:

1. *Department Head/Junior Management*—managing a section within an operating unit, this would equate to the coffee shop manager in a hotel operation or the assistant manager of a fast food operation.
2. *Unit Manager/Section Manager*—managing a complete unit or a section within a larger unit, This would equate to a unit catering manage working for a contract catering company, all executive chef, or the food and beverage manager of a small hotel.
3. *General Manager*—overall control of one large, unit composed of a number of sections or collection of smaller units. This would equal to the food and beverage manager of a large hotel with extensive restaurant, conference and banqueting facilities, or the manager of a small number of catering contracts.
4. *Regional Manager*—overall responsibility for a number of separate large units or geographic areas.

5. *Director*—responsibility for the operation and management of a complete organization

6. *Owner/Proprietor/Partner*—Managing operations recorded the second highest number of incidents across the three sub-categories of managing day-to-day operations, specialist/technical areas and managing crises. The analysis by managerial level, shown above shows a heavy emphasis in this area for the junior managers. This was strongest in day-to-day operations and specialist knowledge but when it came to a crisis the junior managers were more likely to call in their unit or general manager. Owners also get heavily involved in sorting out the crises that may occur within their businesses.

Sector comparisons show that hotels and restaurants reported the heaviest emphasis on managing operations while employee catering had the lowest. The area of managing the business included aspects of managing business performance, managing projects, managing strategic decisions and managing legal complexity. Across the whole sample, this area was in third place behind personal skills and managing operations. More detailed analysis by managerial level reveals some significant differences. Although general managers, regional managers and directors show significantly more incidents in this area, junior managers and unit managers show a low emphasis. This suggests that managers as a whole may be becoming more business oriented but only when they have reached a position of some seniority with an organization. Comparisons across the sectors of the industry reflect this emphasis, with hotels, restaurants and popular catering, sectors with large numbers of junior managers, showing a low emphasis on this area but other sectors, especially contract catering and local authority services, featuring positively. The managing people area covered managing individuals, managing teams, managing external contacts and managing personnel administration. It was therefore surprising that, given the labour intensity of many sectors of the industry and the natural importance given to this area, there were relatively few reported incidents in this area. One explanation for this anomaly is that the interpersonal skills involved in managing people are not included in this section but are categorized as more generic personal skills.

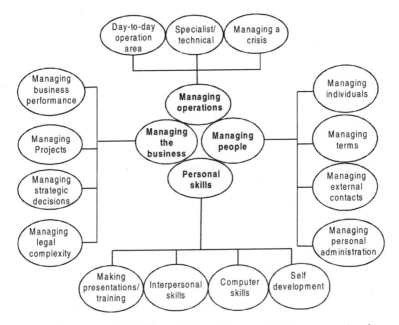

Analysis across managerial level shows unit managers having the highest score in this area with junior managers and owners having low scores. The area of personal skills includes a range of generic or transferable skills that cover making verbal or written presentations, training, inter-personal skills, using computers in management and self development. There were more incidents reported in this area than any other and most of these were in the interpersonal skills area, followed by making presentations and training. Using computers in business showed comparatively few incidents and incidents to do with self-development were sadly, for an industry that seemingly values training highly, very sparse. All levels of manager reported large numbers of incidents in the area of interpersonal skills, especially the junior managers who would be new to having to handle these situations. Again there was an even spread across all sectors of the industry but a heavier than expected emphasis in popular catering or fast food. This is perhaps a reflection of the time managers spend dealing with interpersonal issues when the technological issues have been removed from consideration through systematized service delivery systems.

Responsibilities of Food and Beverage Management

The research described above highlights the areas of activity that all managers are involved in but does not look at the specific responsibilities of the food and beverage manager. The significant contribution food and beverage sales can make towards total sales is evident but food and beverage costs can make equally significant inroads into sales. This necessitates the development of an effective system of control for all areas concerned with the food and beverage function. The development of such a total control system begins with the basic policy decisions described previously the determination of the financial, marketing and catering policies. Working within these three broad policies of the establishment, the food and beverage department is then able to detail its objectives. The main responsibilities and objectives of the food and beverage department may be summarized as follows:

1. The provision of food and beverage products and services catering for clearly defined markets to satisfy or exceed these customers' expectations.
2. The purchasing, receiving, storing, issuing and preparation of food and beverages within the establishment for final provision and service to the customer.

3. The formulation of an efficient control system within the food and beverage department with the purpose of:
   (i) Monitoring food and beverage prices and achieving competitive rates while still ensuring quality standards;
   (ii) Pricing restaurant and special function menus to achieve desired profit margins;
   (iii) Compiling on a daily, weekly and monthly basis, all relevant food and beverage information on costs and sales that may be used by management for forecasting, planning, budgeting, etc.
4. Reconciling actual and forecast costs and sales, and initiating corrective action if discrepancies occur, and finding out and eliminating the causes, for example bad portion; control, incorrect pricing, etc.
5. Training, directing, motivating and monitoring of all food and beverage department staff
6. Co-operating with other departments to become a significant contributor to the organization's short and long-term profitability.
7. Obtaining in a regular, structured and systematic way, feedback from customers, so that their comments, complaints and compliments may be taken into account to improve the overall standard of service.

These are the major responsibilities and objectives of a food and beverage department. Other minor objectives do become important during the day-to-day running of the department, but these often tend to deal with sudden crises or short-term problems and would be too numerous to mention. However, achieving all these objectives is a far from easy task when managers are faced with the inherent complexity and variability of a food and beverage operation.

Constraints on Food and Beverage Management

The management of food and beverage departments has been described as the most technical and complex in the hotel and catering trade. The specific factors that make food and beverage management relatively more complex are due to particular external and internal pressures.

External Factors

The external factors are often seen as the 'major' problems of the food and beverage function. They originate outside the organization and for this reason internal action can rarely solve the problem adequately, although proactive management may help to reduce their impact. Some of the major external pressures affecting the food and beverage function are listed below.

Government/Political

1. Specific government taxes, for example, VAT.
2. Government policies on training and employment, economic development, regional development, etc
3. Government legislation

Economic

1. Rising costs—foods and beverages, labour, fuel, rates and insurance.
2. Sales instability peaks and troughs of activity occur on a daily, weekly and seasonal basis
3. Changes in expenditure patterns and people's disposable incomes
4. Expansion and retraction of credit facilities
5. Interest rates on borrowed capital

Social

1. Changes in population distribution, for example,

population drifting away from certain areas or demographic such as age structure.
2. Changes in the socio-economic groupings of an area
3. Growth of ethnic minorities leading to a demand for more varied foods
4. Changes in food fashion, for example, current popularity of take-away foods, home delivery of fast foods, and trends in healthy eating.

Technical
1. Mechanization, for example, of food production and food service equipment.
2. Information technologies, for example, data processing in hotel and catering establishments.
3. Product developments for example organic vegetables, increased shelf life of foods through irradiation, meat and dairy produce alternatives.

Internal Factors

Along with external factors, the food and beverage function also has many other day-to-day internal pressures. Internal problems are those originating within the organization and for these reason such problems can usually be solved adequately within the establishment if they can be identified and the root cause removed. The internal problems may be classified as follows.

Food and Beverage
1. Perishability of food and the need for adequate stock turnover.
2. Wastage and bad portion control.
3. Pilferage from kitchens, restaurants, bars and stores

Staff
1. General staff shortages and skill shortages within the industry.

2. Staff shortages often coinciding with peaks of sales activity.
3. Conversely, staff surpluses coinciding with troughs in sales activity.
4. Absenteeism, illness, etc.
5. Use of part-time or casual staff in some food and beverage departments.
6. Poor supervision and training of new staff.
7. High staff turns over particularly in some areas.

Control

1. Cash and credit control and collection.
2. Maintenance of all cost in line with budget guidelines and current volume of business
3. Maintenance of a type and efficient control of all food and beverage stocks.
4. Maintenance of up to date costing and pricing of all menu items.
5. Maintenance of an efficient food and beverage control system giving analyzed statistical data of all business done.

There is a dividing line between those food and beverage departments that take a proactive approach to these external and internal problems and hence functioned more efficiently and those that just react to the problems only ever treating the symptoms and not the causes. It is important management identify therefore the potential problem areas in advance so that they can be planned for and successfully managed when they occur. This is possible if there is some form of feed back from the control function back to the management so that they kept constantly aware of changes in food and beverage area and also outside the establishment that may have an effect.

Two

Characteristics of Food and Beverage

Food

The edible parts of plants and animals may be termed as 'food', in so far as people eat them in some form or another to satisfy their physiological, psychological and social needs.

For the purpose of meeting the needs of the body for growth and maintenance, foods have generally been placed into three basic categories referred to as food groups on the basis of the nutrients they supply for the various functions of the body.

These are:

(i) Energy giving
(ii) Body building and maintenance and
(iii) Protective.

A fourth group covering miscellaneous food may be added to this with the purpose of including all those items used in food preparation which enhance the quality and acceptability of food.

It is universally accepted that the nutritional value of food is not primarily what makes people eat. It is its colour, flavour, texture, temperature and presentation. Besides, due to the enormous range of foods which people eat all over the world, there may be some items which do not fall into the three groups, mentioned above, and these can then be accommodated in the miscellaneous group.

These good groups are an excellent aid to planning meals in which nutritional considerations are of primary importance, such as planning for school children, sick or old people, and in general, people who for some reason have become vulnerable to the hazards of nutritional imbalance.

One food taken from each food group at every meal would ensure balance in the plans, not only in terms of nutrients but also colour, texture, flavour and other factors that make food more acceptable and palatable. There is unlimited scope for the development of dishes, through various combinations of food from the different food groups. The figure gives only a few examples of food under each category. These lists can be extended according to availability of similar foods in different countries, regions, climates and seasons. It must however be remembered that every food contains some energy giving, body building and protective elements, and therefore in practice cannot be strictly segregated into well-defined groups.

Types of Foods

As many as 664 types of foods have been listed in India alone, under cereals, pulses, nuts and oil-seeds, vegetables, fruits, milk and milk products and flesh foods. When these are combined in various ways and in different amounts the possibilities are unlimited. Apart from the variety that is possible in food preparation, every food manager must be aware of the types of foods available for use in food services and their seasonal availability. Foods ate generally available in two forms, natural and processed.

Natural Foods

As the term indicates these foods are available in their natural forms as they appear from farms, orchards, slaughterhouses and water sources. Some examples are fresh fruits and vegetables, freshly cut meats, fish, nuts, pulses and legumes as harvested, While the nuts, pulses and legumes can be used in their natural forms, they are generally subjected to some form of processing to enhance their storage life.

Processed Foods

Processed foods are those that have undergone some type of treatment on a small or large scale before they are used as basic ingredients of a meal or consumed as such. Cereal foods are rarely used in their harvested form, and are generally subjected to processing. For example, cereals are milled into flours; broken cereals are used for porridges, semolina, etc. Other foods also vary considerably in the extent to which they are processed. Some synthetically manufactured foods are also marketed which have possibilities in food production, such as essences, emulsifiers, vinegar and so on.

As the variety demanded by customers is increasing, food service managers are turning more and more to processed forms that are time and energy saving in food preparation. The list keeps on expanding with the fast growing technological developments and the changing demands of people and food services. Such foods have been termed as 'convenience foods'. Most fast food outlets depend heavily on the use of convenience foods in the form of proportioned packed cuts of meat, fish and poultry; partly prepared foods to be finished on demand and served; and even ready to serve food straight from cans or packs. Canned and preserved foods form part of every food store in any catering establishment.

Whatever the type of food or form in which ingredients are used, it is important to maintain the quality of whatever is offered to the customer. Foods differ in their qualities form season to season and according to varieties, breeds and feeds. Besides, customers differ widely in their expectations of food. Controlling quality is therefore a great challenge to every caterer irrespective of the nature or size of his food service.

When dealing with food materials and meal preparation for customers. It is hard to define the term 'quality' because it means different things to different people. Quality has defined as the 'degree of excellence' that can be offered to the customer.

Day to day experience shows that whether one pays for tomatoes, apples or a meal, customers do not mind paying more for what they think is better quality food or service. The factors that make food more acceptable are chiefly those that directly affect palatability of meals.

From the point of view of the caterer, however, 'quality' not only includes palatability characteristics (which though important can be enhanced or masked as desired, by the use of additives), but the production of meals that are wholesome in terms of their being safe for consumption. Nothing is more detrimental to a food service organization than a case of food poisoning among its customers. Obviously, it does not signify the most superior or best grade, so some means need to be devised to decide on where to draw the line in terms of selecting ingredients, and methods of putting them together to suit the expectations of the customers. Thus, it is necessary to lay down standards for each of the qualities and be able to control them at every stage of the production cycle.

Quantitative Aspects of Quality

For the caterer it provides a means of control over costs and by controlling portions, numbers, weight and volume while for the customer it indicates 'value for money'.

Number: Controlling numbers is just a matter of counting correctly, and with proper supervision is an easy task. It can be done manually or mechanically e.g. one small cake per person, or 100 doughnuts from one kilogram of dough, prepared by a doughnut machine of that capacity.

Weight or Volume: Standards for weights and volumes of different ingredients and dishes can be established by the use of scales, slicing machines, measuring equipment, scoops and ladles designed to hold a measured weight or volume of food. For example, one scoop of ice cream may be exactly 25 or 30 grams by weight. Some weight and volume equipment commonly used and found suitable for even the smallest food service operation.

Table 2.1: Standard Cup and Spoon Equivalents

Standard Cup	Standard Spoon	Volume of Contents (ml)	Remarks
1	50	250	
4/5	40	200	Household containers may be standardized using the standard equipment.
3/5	30	150	
1/2	25	125	
2/5	20	100	
1/5	10	50	

One standard cup is equivalent to 50 standard spoons that are both equal to 250 ml in volume.

Very after to speed up service, measuring against standards or by standardizes teacups or other common use equipment experience. Household equipment may be standardized by using standard equipment for measuring ingredients or portions in small establishments such as in kiosks, tea stalls, coffee shops where space restrictions and costs inhibit the purchase of standard weighing and measuring equipment.

Table gives some standard cup and spoon equivalents of some foods commonly used-in food preparation.

Table 2.2: Standard Cup and Spoon Equivalents of Some Foods

Standard Cup	Weight (g)	Standard Spoon (g)	Weight (g)
Cereals			
Rice	200	Sodium bicarbonate	4.4
Semolina (fine)	160	Gingelly seed	4.0
Semolina (coarse)	250	Jaggery	4.0
Jowar	110	Salt	6.0
Refined flour	121	Sugar	3.0
Maize	160	Oil	5.0
Ragi	180		
Wheat	125		
Groundnut	125		
Pulses			
Bengal gram	180		
Others	125		
Milk			
Buffalo	243		
Cow	246		
Dry skimmed	131		
Dry whole	200		
Sugar	161		
Water	250		

In addition, small establishments are often busy places, especially if located on railway platforms, bus stations, at fairs, etc. and use of the available equipment for measuring out portions in quicker than using a standard spoon every time salt or sugar has to be added to food. Table gives some weight equivalents determined by the use of cups, tumblers, bowls, etc. often used in food services.

Table 2.3: Weight Equivalents of Daily Use Equipment

Equipment Wt	Equivalents (g)	Remarks
Teacup	200	
Steel tumbler	375	
Glass tumbler	265	Water was used to established the weight volume measurements ml of water as equivalent to 1 gm.
Coconut shell	275	
Mud Vessel	250	
Empty cheese tin	300	

The shape of foods can be controlled by the use of moulds, trays and tins or by using grading machines that provide standard sizes and shapes in terms of accepted portions. For example, dough cutters, jelly moulds, cake tins, etc.

The accuracy and sophistication used in controlling portions depends greatly on the volume of production. The larger the volume, the greater would be the degree of mechanization or automation used in controlling quantity. It is for this reason that a lot of portion controlling has shifted to the manufacturer's domain, from where due to the large volumes produced, the sizes, shapes, weights, volumes, numbers and even costs can be controlled with greater accuracy. This also enables the smaller food establishments to buy food that has been proportioned, and then prepare and serve them to the customer. Examples of shape standardizations are seen in sausages, portioned chops, fillets, cans with the exact number and size of slices in them for corresponding net weight.

Sensory Quality

This refers to those characteristics of food that can be identified by use of our senses such as, appearance, smell, taste, feel and sound of food.

Appearance

It is common experience that if food does not look good when served, it will be rejected even if its taste is good. So the most important feature of food acceptability is its appearance, which is largely contributed by is the colour and texture of foods selected and their presentation to the customer.

Colour

Foods get their colour in many different ways:

(a) From natural plant and animal pigments;
(b) From the effect of heat on sugar in foods,
(c) Chemical reactions between sugars and proteins, and
(d) The oxidation of chemical compounds present in foods.

Natural Plant and Animal Pigments

There are a number of pigments present naturally in plant and animal tissues, which are sensitive to physical and chemical changes. Foods therefore tend to change their colours with the degree of handling, exposure to air, sunlight and different temperatures used in the process of cooking. In the process of chopping, grating and grinding, the colours also get affected, because the cells or chloroplasts containing them get damaged releasing the pigments. Once released contact with air further destroys them.

Effect of Heat on Sugars

Sugars when heated turn brown and caramelize, imparting a brown colour to foods that contain them as in the colour of candies, toasted bread and caramelized fruits.

Chemical Reactions

The amino group from proteins in foods combines with the

aldehyde or ketone groups from carbohydrate or sugar molecules and lead to the darkening of foods. This is generally called 'Maillard browning' as in the case of milk heated for a long time to thicken or condense it. Examples of this type of non-enzymatic browning are seen on the surface of baked dishes and roasted meats or nuts.

Oxidation

Foods contain certain chemicals that on contact with air get converted to their oxidized forms imparting colour to foods. Examples include the darkening of cut fruits and vegetables when exposed to air such as apples, bananas, brinjals, pears, potatoes, etc. Also tea turns darker on keeping. These reactions get accelerated in the presence of metallic ions like iron and copper, as seen when fruits are cut with iron knives or vegetables are cooked in iron or copper pans. The colour of cooked foods may be due to the above factors working singly or in combination during the different stages of food preparation, cooking and service.

Colour is also associated with the degree of ripeness, flavour, taste, concentration of food and the degree of 'doneness', etc, all of which determine acceptability. In short, the form in which the food is presented influences choice. Also menus that show a variety in colour and form are highly acceptable.

Flavor

Once the eyes are satisfied with the quality, the sensory organs of the nose and mouth take over. What is called 'flavour' of foods then affects the customer. Flavour relates to the combined sensation of odour or aroma, taste and the feel of food in the mouth. Several compounds present in foods are responsible for flavour and aroma. These substances are very sensitive to oxidation and high temperatures, and tend to interact with each other. It is for this reason that flavours change with time and temperature. With very few exceptions, flavours generally deteriorate with handling, processing and storage; therefore no food tastes as good as fresh food. The terms 'farm fresh' or straight from the fire or 'just baked' are only too familiar, as far as attracting customers is concerned. No wonder a small kiosk where juice is freshly extracted for each customer, is generally overcrowded, in contrast to one where bottled or canned juice is served.

Flavour acceptance or rejection, however, is also influenced by people's cultural, regional and religious backgrounds. For instance, a person from western, far eastern or Muslim countries would relish the delicate flavour of beef, as against an Indian who would consider the odour unacceptable simply because the two have different eating habits and experiences with food. The age-old proverb 'one man's meat is another man's poison' is so apt when dealing with food acceptances. These differences have given rise to specialty menus such as Chinese, Continental, and Vegetarian South Indian, and so on, to suit the tastes and values of different people and account for regional and cultural preferences. Large food service establishments offer choices from all these types of menus, while smaller ones cater to single specialties inviting those who would relish particular flavours.

The part that odours play in food acceptability is clear from the fact that very often odours put people off a food even without their tasting it. Odours can be described as pungent, minty, putrid, and so on. Pleasant odours generally result from subtle combinations that are delicate and not strong.

Taste

After the odour is accepted the next sensory test of quality is the taste, that is, the reaction of the taste buds to the food, determining whether it is sweet, sour, salty or bitter. Most foods contain a mixture of some or all the sensations of taste. Acceptability of the food therefore depends on how well they harmonize to make the net sensation pleasurable.

Mouth Feel

The next component of flavour is 'mouthfeel'. Depending on how the food feels in the mouth it may be rejected or enjoyed. The most attractive dishes with pleasant odours and tastes can be rejected if they contain too many chillies or spices that irritate the membranes of the mouth. If the food fe too not in terms of temperature, it causes blisters or pain. Again, the most favourite foods can be rejected if they are too slippery, sticky or hard to bite into.

Texture

Texture of a food can be determined both by perception and mouth-feel. It varies from food to food and in the same food too when different methods of cooking are used. For example, a baked pudding will have a firmer texture than the same pudding if steamed. Texture also depends on the structural composition of food. This quality can be described as rough, smooth, grainy, coarse, fine, crisp, viscous, spongy and heavy. For want of accurate descriptions sometimes analogues are used to describe texture. For instance, a custard may be described as 'creamy' indicating that it is smooth flowing like cream, and not because it has cream in it. Also, cereal preparations like rice or semolina puddings cooked beyond the gelling point may be described as 'gluey' People accept or reject foods that do not agree with their own mental image regarding shape, size, viscosity or sheen. For instance, rice that is overcooked and therefore sticky instead of grainy (with each grain well separated), will not be accepted if customers have a choice. Similarly, a glossy well-set caramel pudding would be in great demand.

Mental Response

Apart from the sensory quality of food, certain psychological factors related to people's experiences with food play an important role in their acceptability. There is an example of a woman who could never accept stuffed brinjals no matter how deliciously they were prepared. This is because she was reminded of a pickle that had once appeared on her table and contained an accidentally pickled rat, which resembled the stuffed brinjal. In contrast, whenever a cake is served it is accepted by people with a feeling of celebration, because of its association with birthdays and weddings.

The mind thus acts as a sensory organ influencing food acceptability. The sense of hunger too is the mental interpretation of a physiological need for food. Conversely we tend to eat a favourite food even when we are not hungry. Such eating expresses our 'appetite' for food which can be called the 'hunger of the mind' and not of the body.

Sound

Besides the mental responses to food, people also exhibit a certain degree of sound sensitivity. For instance, the crackling of spitfires when barbecue drippings fall in them, produce joyful expectancy of freshly cooked food from fire to plate. A similar pleasant reaction occurs when sizzling food is brought for service.

Nutritional Quality

The nutritional quality desired for different food services would vary according to the needs of particular customers, but general guidelines can be established to provide standards that the caterer can follow.

The criteria that may be used are:

  (i) Portion size
 (ii) Seasonal foods
(iii) Wholesome ingredients
(iv) Storage preparation and cooking methods
 (v) Holding and Service methods.

Portion Size

Although the actual amounts of various nutrients present in different foods vary, the weight and or volume of a portion of food served is a fairly good guide to providing nutritional quality. Therefore, it is important to determine standard serving portions for most dishes and further control them by weighing or measuring accurately.

Table 2.4: Standard Serving Portions of Some Dishes

Dish	Portion Size (Wt/Volume)	Indication on Portion Size
Soup	250 ml	1 soup bowl 1 or 2 ladles (No. 2)
Rice	100-150 g	2 ladle No. 1
Vegetables	50-75 g	1 ladle No. 1
Meat	50-75 g	two chops
Fish	50-75 g	two fillets
Chicken	200-250 g	2 pieces
Curry	200-250 g	1 bowl
Sauce	50 m	1 ladle
Cake	50 g	1 piece
Snacks	50-100 g	2 pieces

The accuracy with which portions are measured will depend on the catering situation. For instance, foods and ingredients would have to be actually weighed accurately if the catering is done for hospital patients MI special diets, whereas, for normal people suitable standard sized equipment may be used to regulate the size of portions. This can be done through the use of already measured daily use equipment, like cups that hold 200 ml of tea or mugs holding 300 ml. The portion size used will depend on pricing and other policies of individual establishments.

The latter method is useful for portioning at the point of service, where exact measurements using standard equipment, would give the impression of being stingy, an impression not desirable for good customer relations. Other advantages of using cup or spoon measures are that the service is quicker, and tie quality better. This is so especially if hot beverages like tea, coffee or soup are being portioned, which would get cold if each cup were to be measured with standard equipment and then served. The best way a standardize portion is to buy proportioned food or make suitable portions during food preparation. Many foods lend themselves to such treatment. Examples are equal sizes of cutlets, meatballs, chicken legs (drumsticks), chops, kebabs, chappatis, puris, and so on.

Since quite a number of foods cannot be bought proportioned, particularly for Indian cuisine, or portioned in kitchens, other aids have to be developed to portion such foods using standard and other methods.

Standard Recipes

These are used to ensure that the same ingredients by weight or volume are used every time a dish is cooked. The method of preparation should also be standardized so that the portions obtained each time are consistent in size, shape, volume and colour. Special attention is necessary in the use of garnishes, which, because of the small quantities required tend to be used impulsively without realizing that the cost of the dish can be adversely affected.

Portioning Guides

These are charts indicating portion sizes of items on the menu and are displayed in kitchens and at service points, where staff dishing out or serving the food can refer to them, when in doubt.

Portioning guides are helpful because while kitchens staff may have some idea of portions the service personnel are not always aware of them and may tend to serve unequal portions to customers unintentionally. The manner in which portion sizes are written should be clear to the server.

Close Supervision

This is vital as far as portion control is concerned, because it is at the service point that the costing of dishes gets disturbed. If correct service equipment is supplied and good habits of serving developed, supervision effort gets greatly reduced.

Thus portion control reflects adequate quantities served in relation to different types of dishes, thereby affecting the amount of food sewed and its nutritional quality. Controlling portions does not imply sewing smaller or variable portions, as these not only affect the nutritional quality intended but also jeopardize the 'goodwill' of customers, which is important for the success of any enterprise.

Seasonal Foods

The second criterion for maintaining nutritional quality is the use of seasonal foods in meal preparation. This is because in season foods are best in their nutritive content particularly vitamin C and B-complex vitamins. In addition, fruits and vegetables particularly, are best in colour, flavour, and size in the prime of their season, in contrast to off-season produce.

As far as fish and seafood are concerned, it is advisable not to consume them during breeding seasons because of the presence of certain non-nutritional factors and substances, which are toxic in their effects on the human system.

General Guideline Principle

Never prepare or serve fresh fish in-those months which do not contain the letter R, because these months in India (May to August) coincide with breeding seasons and are also monsoon leading to contamination of water in ponds and rivers with fisheries developing in the country however, fish and seafood in frozen packs or in dehydrated forms are now available for consumption throughout the year, especially in the metropolitan cities. In developed countries where fishing is done under controlled conditions and the catch transported immediately for processing and preservation. The season is not of much significance. The same holds good when dealing with meat and meat products that are available in processed forms.

Fortunately, the nutritive content of meat products does not vary greatly with time and season. It is more affected by the breed, the feed and the environmental conditions in which the animals are reared.

Wholesome Ingredients

This criterion refers to the quality of ingredients used in food production, and without doubt, different varieties, sizes and maturity levels have different nutritive values. Besides the presence of essential nutrients, wholesomeness also signifies freedom from contamination, infection and toxicity. This is generally taken care of through hygienic and sanitary practices in the handling of foods at every stage of production, service and the disposal of waste materials. Wholesomeness of individual foods has its 'effects on the dishes prepared from them.

Wholesomeness is the primary consideration for nutritional quality of dishes prepared, but it is worth mentioning that sometimes the sizes of irregular shape of foods do detract from its wholesomeness. While selecting foods therefore, the end use to which they are going to be put is an important consideration.

Table 2.5: Food Selection Guide

Fresh Foods	Indicators of Wholesomeness
Meat	Age of animal seen from skeleton and colour of muscle desirable colour red to pink.
Processed Meat	Cans check for date of manufacture frozen check date of manufacture.
Fish	Body firm, scales hard to remove fresh odour bulging eyes red gills.
Poultry	Good overall shape meaty fresh odour.
Milk and Milk Product	Good colour opaque well sealed bottles or packs. No odour uncurded.
Eggs	Smooth velvety surface no cracks clean shell.
Fruits and Vegetables	Natural colour firm evenly shaped matured seasonal free from dirt.
Cereals, Pulses, Legumes, Nuts	Free from insect infestation stones or other adulterations.
Fats and Oils	No rancidity oils free flowing properly sealed containers.
Packed and Bottled food	Cans not dented packs not torn, bottles and jars sealed air tight.

For the sake of convenience the following menu has been taken as the starting point:

1. Soup
2. Chicken Preparation
3. Fried Rice
4. Mint Raita (Chopped mint in beaten curd or yogurt)
5. Salad
6. Fresh Fruit

Soup

When ingredients are selected for the preparation of soups the points to consider are flavour and colour, while size and shape of the foods is of little significance. Even unblemished peelings of seasonal peas, carrots, beet greens the end parts from sliced onions and tops of spring onion, which would normally be discarded while preparing vegetables, may be thoroughly washed and added to the stock pot to extract maximum flavour and colour. In their prime, vegetables and fruits have good colour, flavour and nutritive value even if they are small in size and irregular in shape.

If meats are used for stocks, all trimmings well washed may be added along with bones from boned meats for maximum flavour and nutrition. The additional advantage lies in making maximum use of food materials and lowering costs, while still maintaining the taste, flavour, wholesomeness and presentation of the food.

Chicken Preparation

This being a main dish, it requires selection of meaty good sized pieces. If the selection is to be made for a curry, the chicken may be cut into 8 to 10 pieces in contrast to 4 or 6 pieces for making "tandoori" or roast chicken. In fact, for the latter, even the whole bird dressed and drawn may be used. One chicken would normally provide four portions of curry. Broilers are better and quicker to cook, thereby providing better nutritional quality.

Fried Rice

This is generally referred to as 'pulao' in India, each variety named after the ingredients used in the rice preparation. The quality of the rice is extremely important, and a good pulao requires long grain-matured rice, which has a subtle flavour. Old rice makes better pulaos than newly harvested grains. The 'basmati' variety of rice is well known for its superior flavour and size of grain, both ideals for pulao. The quality or rice selected will, however, differ if Chinese fried rice is to be prepared; in this case the small grain variety is preferred.

Mint Raita

This is a popular side dish served with main meals, especially with rice, in India. The 'raita' is whipped cured or yogurts into which mint or other ingredients are added. Traditionally, curds are prepared from milk in most food services and not bought pre packed. The quality of the set, however, depends on the starter and the type of milk used, homogenized, and standard or whole milk giving well set curds. Skimmed milk tends to give watery curds, though the nutritional quality is not appreciably affected except in terms of what milk fat contributes (energy and vitamin A). For raitas the taste of curd is more important than the firmness of the set. This is because the Curd has in any case to be whipped to destroy the set. The curd must not be too sour and a 'mint' raita must have the characteristic flavour and colour of fresh mint. The size of the mint leaf is of little significance in its selection, since it has to be ground or chopped fine before adding it to the curd.

Salad

Since salad ingredients are not generally cooked except beetroot (which may be steamed) selection needs to be done with care.

(a) Tomatoes must be orange-red, regular in shape, firm an unblemished.

(b) Lettuce and other greens need to be crisp, bright and free from any signs of insect infestation.

(c) Carrots should be orange to red, firm, but young and slightly sweet to taste.

(d) If meat, cheese or egg salads are prepared, the quality should be the best, because salads when held for service cannot be done at freezing or boiling temperatures. Salads left unused should generally be given away and never reused if they are high protein salads containing chicken, meat or fish.

The wholesomeness of salads therefore, depends on their freshness, the degree of cooking of meat and eggs to make them safe, the conditions of the cans if canned meats are used. It is preferable to use roasted meats for salads, because flavours get sealed into the meats better, the colour is improved and the danger of contamination is minimized.

Fresh Fruit

Seasonal varieties having good colour, size and regular shape characteristic of the fruit, neejl to be selected for dessert fruit. Fruits always have full flavor and just ripe taste when in season. If the fruit cut and served as mixed fruit salad, or as an ingredient in puddings, then smaller sizes and misshapen fruits having full colour, flavor, and taste may be used without hesitation.

Storage, Preparation and Cooking Methods

The storage, preparing and cooking methods used, greatly enhance, retain or mar the nutritional quality of the food. This is because different nutrients vary in their physical and chemical properties, some being water soluble, others fat-soluble, some table others unstable to heat, light, acids, alkalis and oxygen.

The conditions of storage like temperature, humidity, lighting (natural or otherwise), ventilation, sanitation, method and length of storage and the wholesomeness of the food at the time of storage, all affect its nutritive value. It is therefore advisable to use foods, particularly perishable ones as soon as they are received, considering that before they rich the food service establishment they have already undergone a lot of handling, storage and exposure to environmental conditions.

The preparation of food prior to cooking also brings about changes in nutritional quality. Peeling, trimming, cutting and washing of foods affects its nutrient content as indicated in table.

Table 2.6: Effect of preparation procedure on the Nutritive Value of Foods

Preparation	Method of Work	Effect on Nutrients	Retention Method
Peeling	Removing peels, food expose to air.	Vitamin A and C lost.	Use food with peels as far as possible.
Washing	Washing after peeling and cutting.	Soluble Vitamins washed out.	Minimize washing.
Cutting	Size of cut large or small.	Large pieces result in less losses.	Cook whole if possible.

Table only emphasizes the losses that take place of vitamins that are present in large amounts in fresh fruits and vegetables that are usually peeled, washed and then cooked or eaten as such. These nutrients get further destroyed when the food is subjected to heat in cooking. Besides the vitamins, mineral elements are also washed away in the form of salts that easily dissolve in water. IT is not always possible to estimate the exact extent of the loss unless the cooked food is subjected to laboratory analysis and the nutrients present determined exactly. This is, however not feasible in food service establishments, but guide to enable nutritionally effective procedures to be established in kitchens and service areas can be formulated, as given below:

(a) Separate areas for preparing food from those of cooking to prevent cross-contamination.

(b) Use minimum amount of water in cooking food to prevent water-soluble nutrients from dissolving out.

(c) Cook food in the shortest possible, time to protect heat labile B-complex vitamins and certain minerals, which can form insoluble compounds and precipitate out becoming unavailable to the body. Longer cooking times can destroy essential amino acids to the extent of 30-100 per cent.

(d) Cooking at very high temperatures should be avoided because even some of the heat stable nutrients can be destroyed. The method of cooking best suited for a particular food should be used for it.

(e) Any water used in cooking should never be discarded, but made use of in gravies, sauces soups, etc.

(f) Serve food as soon after cooking as possible.

In general, moist methods of cooking have less drastic effects on nutrients than dry methods provided no lunched out liquid is discarded. For high protein foods like meat, eggs, cheese, etc., dry methods are suitable as the protein coagulates fast enough to seal the nutrients in the food.

In food services, because large volumes of food are handled and cooked to have them ready to serve on demand, losses in nutrients also take place during the period of holding the food. This is because heat is constantly applied to the equipment to keep the food hot. Temperatures need to be monitored very carefully for proper nutrient retention and safety of the food.

Holding and Service Methods

In food service establishments it is imperative to hold food for varying periods in anticipation of customer demand. Depending on the acidity or alkalinity of the food, nutrient losses take place. At a neutral pH of 7 most nutrients are stable except ascorbic acid (Vitamin C), folic acid and thiamin. At acid pH (less than 7), Vitamin A, carotenes, some B-vitamins and amino acids get unstable, though vitamin C becomes more stable. In an alkaline medium (more than pH 7) vitamin C becomes unstable and some B-vitamins get destroyed. In the presence of oxygen essential amino acids degenerate, so do vitamins B_1 and B_2 (thiamine and riboflavin). In the presence of sunlight too riboflavin, carotenes, vitamin A and vitamin C get affected.

The losses of nutrients are proportional to the time of holding and the temperatures at which the food is held. Most foods must be held above 63°C to make them microbiologically safe. Holding time and temperatures not only affect the nutritional quality, but also the sensory and quantities quality of foods. The sensory qualities are affected due to chemical and non-enzymatic reactions taking place in the food; volatilization of flavor substances and changes in texture because of being heated over long periods. The nutritional quality of foods is also affected by the methods chosen for service. Those requiring food to be exposed for a long time before it is consumed lead to oxidative changes and consequent losses, as compared to those served and eaten as soon as they are prepared.

Having identified some of the factors which affect nutritional quality it is worth mentioning that some methods can be used to retain or even enhance nutritive quality in the process of food preparing indicates these briefly.

Table 2.7: Improving Nutritive Quality of Foods

Methods	Food	Effect on Quality
Germination	Pulses, cereals, legumes	Improves level of B-vitamins and the Biological value of proteins in some pulses. Vitamin C is developed.
Fermentation	Pulse-cereal mixtures, breads.	B-vitamin content is enhanced especially with yeast fermentation.
Supplementation	Foods cooked in combination, such as cereal-vegetable, cereal-milk, cereal-pulse, cereal-egg or meat, fruit-milk, etc.	The nutrients lacking in one food get provided by the other food Fruit and milk provides protein.
Fortification	Flour, fats and oils, salt, milk, etc.	Nutrients are added to foods after or in the process of manufacture to improve their nutritional quality.
Enrichment	Flour and its products, canned foods, etc.	Nutrients added to food by manufacturers to make up the losses that have taken place during processing.

Methods of retaining nutritive value are those involving short cooking time, low temperatures, acid medium and use of the cooking liquid. If it cannot be used as such, it may be incorporated as an ingredient in another dish. A good example is when milk is split to make cottage cheese, which separates out may be used for making dough for roti, poori, naan, etc. Alternatively, it may be used instead f water to make a rice preparation or a curry.

In the case of convenience foods the nutritive value is generally given on the packages of foods marketed, from which the nutritive quality can be ascertained.

Having discussed the quality characteristics in relation to acceptability it is necessary to emphasize that the quality to be served must be acceptable to both the customer and the food service establishment. The latter may not always decide to serve the most 'superior' quality but the 'best' possible within its cost structure and the level of customer demand. All the qualities of food must therefore necessarily fall within affordable costs for the establishment and the paying power of the customer.

Table 2.8: Expenditure on Different Food Categories in an Establishment

Food Group	Proportion of Total Food Cost (%)
Meats	25-30
Milk and milk products	15-20
Vegetables and fruits	10-20
Cereals	10-15
Fats and sweets	10-20
Miscellaneous	50-10

Using the above guidelines the following example will illustrate in actual money value, the amounts to be spent on each category of foods.

The quality of a dish or meal is determined by the quality of the ingredients used in its preparation. In general, proper attention to controlling portions in terms of weights and volumes at appropriate stages of the production cycle will take care of the quality characteristics aimed at. This is because if ingredients are mixed together accurately by standard methods one can reproduce the same flavours, textures, colours and portions acceptable to both customers and management.

The maintenance of quality, however, also requires adherence to the food laws and those regarding hygiene and sanitation and the development of clean working habits.

Quality Control Procedures

Quality control procedures adopted by various establishments differ according to the size of the operation. Smaller establishments require less sophisticated methods than larger ones that handle greater volumes of food, and therefore face greater chances of contamination if handled traditionally. If machinery not used to speed up the work and reduce the amount of exposure of food to air and handling, it would difficult to control quality.Quality Control Procedures Basically Involve Three Steps:

Setting Out Accurate Specifications for Each Food

This is done to communicate to the supplier the exact sizes, weights, numbers, etc. required. Sometimes, descriptions or coloured pictures of products may be used. This may also be displayed at different preparation centers in kitchens to guide staff to produce dishes that match them in their quality characteristics.

Sample specifications appear in the following table:

Product	Quantity/ Pack	Av. Wt. (gm)	Colour of Shell	Freshness	Interior Quality
Eggs	2.5 Doz./ Tray Carton of 6 Trays	50-60	White/ Brown	Not over 4 days after laying	Tested by candling yolk in the center. Thick gelatinous white
Price Rs............ Per day.............					
Additional information.....................Deliver two cartons on................Date					
Use in preparation............................For breakfast preparations, and in puddings, cakes/biscuits/All.					

In India there is no official system of grading eggs unlike in the developed countries, where they are marked AA, A, B and so on. But vendors do grade them visually by size and colour and price them separately. In such conditions it is important to buy from farm sources reputed vendors who will contract r replacing the number of eggs delivered spoilt. In tropical countries weather conditions also contribute to spoilage easily arid therefore it is a greater challenge to the caterer to provide exact specifications and conditions of supply, to maintain a quality service.

In catering establishments, the development of specifications is very important because those who receive the goods are not food specialists. The store staffs commonly check what is delivered with the delivery note and match it with the order placed by the catering manager.

Specifications help staff to check foods received more thoroughly for the quality required.

Checking Foods for Quality

Each food needs to be checked for quality against the specifications desired. This is done when the foods are received so that any item that does not conform to the specified quality is not accepted. Sometimes, due to carelessness or ignorance of staff, quality of foods may get compromised leading to spoilage in storage and losses. Specifications can also be developed for foods in process and those completed for service, to enable staff to check quality at strategic points in the production process. For instance, laying down standards for the thickness of the peel to be removed in preparing vegetables and fruits; checking to see that any equipment used is cleaned immediately to remove debris remaining in the machine; using the correct method of cooking for a food to avoid undue losses in nutritional, organoleptic and other qualities, and finally checking the temperatures of holding equipment. At the service point also quality can be checked in terms of portion served, temperature of the food, its consistency and garnishing.

Testing the Finished Product

The importance of testing the finished product before it is presented to the customer cannot be over emphasized. All testing should focus on those aspects of quality which are of concern to the customer and make food acceptable to him, such as appearance, palatability, portion and so on. This is because the idea is to see all food prepared for service as far as possible.

A Sample Specification Performa for a Prepared Dish

Dish	Appearance	Odour/Taste	Texture	Composition	Presentation	Portion
Picture or Description						

Remarks: Mention any defects or give suggestions for improving any of the qualities in the dish under test.

If on testing a dish for quality, it is found to be unacceptable in any way, immediate action should be taken to prevent it from being served to the customer. The process involved in its preparation, and the quality of ingredients used must be re-examined and any identifiable defects removed. It is wrong policy to camouflage defects in a dish by addition of excess flavourings or colours before serving it to customers.

While quality control is essential for every food service operation, one must not be too carried away with tests considering that quality procedures are time consuming and costly. The question then arises as to how much time, energy and money should be spent on them. This is difficult to slate in concrete terms, because it must vary with the type of foods and the manner in which they are being handled. The sales volume is, however, a good guide to customer acceptability of the food.

Foods Recommended for Use in Canteens, Lunch Rooms and Kiosks

The foods recommended for service in the different establishments are based on a number of factors:

(a) Expectations of the customer and his paying power.
(b) Location of the food service facility.
(c) Size of the establishment.
(d) Hours during which it is open for service.
(e) Type of storage facilities available
(f) Type of establishment and service style

Canteens

The foods suitable for service in canteens are hot and cold beverages, snacks both light and meaty, plated; meals, sweets or desserts, depending on where the canteen is located and who the customers are, denoting; their food habits, needs and purchasing power.

Office canteen: An office canteen which would be required to cater to officers of all ranks and occasionally be called upon to cater for functions or buffet lunches should have the facilities for providing complete meal in the form of a table d'hote menu, and snacks varying from pakoras (fritters) and peanuts cakes, biscuits and sandwiches with tea, coffee and bottled or canned drinks. Such a range of foods would provide the necessary choices for people who would want a substantial meal to those who only wish supplement their packed lunches. All during tea and coffee breaks requires hot and cold beverages, with or without a snack so every canteen must have these on the menu. Some may have important guests to entertain at work for who ready snacks like cake, sandwiches, etc. should be available. At the same time, choices should enable items mixed, matched and finished on demand, so that the food is fresh when served. Holding or reheating food makes it unpalatable and dangerous, because canteens have limited usage facilities and unpredictable demand.

College or School Canteen

The foods suitable for college or school canteens would preferably include nutritious and satisfying snacks, tidbits, 'chaat' and hot and cold beverages to suit the taste of the customers. For example, children's favourites to include would be chowmien, pizzas, samosa, dosa, lana, poori, fried snacks like cutlets and kebabs, small cakes, patties, burgers, milk shakes, juices, aerated inks, packeted nuts, popcorn and wafer. Fresh fruits would also be a good item. In short, students expect foods that are quick to eat, not elaborate or messy, but attractive and appetizing.

Industrial Employee Canteen

These cater to the workforce mainly, though a minority of senior staff may order lunches or teas and snacks to be served to them in management dining rooms, or in their offices.

The food is generally served plated in 'thalis', the table d'hote menu taking the form of chappati, ice, one curry, one seasonal sautéed vegetable, onion and green chili or seasonal salad. Sweet and desserts may be made available but priced separately for those who wish to pay for them.

In employee canteens, any foods placed on the menu would take care of nutritional and satiety factors, s canteen meals and snacks provide the main food for the factory workers. This is because they would like to take advantage of the subsidized meals provided at work as a welfare measure. In addition the work force is employed for the work round the clock, and those on night shifts take heavy breakfast in canteens before going off duty, while those on day duty necessarily work through lunch or dinner times and eat lain meals in the canteen.

Public Canteens

These may be situated at market places or shopping centers, trade fairs, bus stations, airports, other ports, railway stations or wherever customers represent the public masses. These are also called snack bars when they offer food items that are snaky in nature, whether plated or sold as individual items. In addition, they generally provide beverages, both hot and cold or even desserts and ice creams. The latter may be situated at airports where customers (passengers) are multinational and refer to stay at the airports between flights.

The types of foods are generally finger foods, but cutlery is available for those who wish to use it. Examples of foods recommended are burger, sandwiches, cookies, cakes, biscuits, pies, pastries, salads and pasta dishes. Canteens at other locations may offer chana-poori, curry-rice, dosa-chutney or sambar with idli and vada, chops with vegetables and so on. Canteens located at bus or railway stations will tend to offer cheaper foods as compared to those at shopping centers, fairs, and airports, to cater to the paying power and tastes of the masses traveling by bus and rail respectively.

As the demand fluctuates quite a bit during the course of the day, it will be noticed that the foods commended are such as will not spoil easily at ordinary temperatures possible for the storage and service f food. The only precaution to take is not to include those items on the menu that are milk or cream based if refrigeration facilities are not feasible, as at bus stations. In addition, foods suggested can mostly be part prepared or prepared wholly and kept ready to serve on demand during times of rush. Also public canteens are exposed to environmental conditions of dust, flies, and which require food to be strictly guarded, against contamination.

Lunch Rooms

Lunchrooms may be rooms attached to offices meant for serving meals to executives; rooms where lunch served to school children in a boarding school; rooms catering to inmates of residence halls on university campuses; or simply a classroom, corridor or verandah of a government rural or urban school serving mid-day meals to children, who may or may not be able to eat two square meals a day at home for various reasons.

It will be appreciated that according to the environment, the size of the establishment, lunchroom and the type of customer, the foods served will vary considerably. What is recommended though, is based on the fact that all lunchrooms catering to schoolchildren need necessarily to keep the nutritional quality of the food as their chief objective.

1

Executives would be expected to come for lunch in a staggered manner, so it recommended that foods that cannot be reheated easily or finished on demand should not be placed on the menu. Executives with their routine work pressures would like to eat their lunch leisurely, and therefore a complete meal is recommended for them and not a snaky one. They are also expected to belong to an age group that would appreciate food items that are traditionally familiar to them. So foods recommended are regional, traditional foods presented in a familiar manner.

In India a typical menu would be:

- ❖ Curry
- ❖ Side vegetable dish
- ❖ Curd or its preparation
- ❖ Rice/cereal preparation like roti, naan, poori, etc.
- ❖ Sweet
- ❖ Accompaniments: salad, papad and pickles.

In case an executive is entertaining colleague from other countries, the menu may be adapted to their needs by including a soup or starter, and serving the meal course by course or as a buffet with seating arrangements. The dessert may be chosen according to the tastes of the guests. In general the food prepared would carry less spices because foreigners are not used to highly spiced foods. In addition, the customers are mostly middle-aged; therefore lightly cooked food using limited cooking fat or cream would be in order. Thus executive lunchrooms would cater to flexible menus according to customer requirements, regional and seasonal variations and so on.

School Lunch Rooms

In boarding schools, children from well-to-do homes generally reside, and therefore the facilities expected are those capable of providing full three or four course meals and snacks with tea or milk in the evenings after play.

School lunchrooms are characterized by large numbers of hungry over-active children (unless they are sick). Therefore, while all meals need to be planned so that they are nutritionally balanced, the selections must enable children to eat quickly, provide satiety value, and enjoyment. With school children burgers (ham, cheese, vegetable, meat) and pizzas are favourites, but while these could form part of the meal platter they should not substitute the meal. Meals can be completed as follows:

❖ Hamburger or Pizza
❖ Roast potatoes/sauté d potatoes
❖ Salad
❖ Fruit yogurt or milk shake

Similarly, pizza may be provided at teatime, as a substantial snack. To shorten the time of service, counter service is the most suitable with arrangements made for seating and dining comfortably. This has two advantage firstly, when children take the tray for self service, as soon as they enter the lunchroom, they feel they are close to food so they do not get too impatient even if they have to queue up. Secondly, they can see the meal on the plates of other children, and on the counter and make their selections before hand. Food well displayed and plated by staff behind the counter enhances the appetite of the children too. In school lunchrooms food may be served in steel 'thalis' or plates that the children carry to their tables and eat from. If rectangular ones are used these act as the trays as well. Once the children have started their meal it is good policy not to disturb them again for second helpings from the counter. Additional bowls of main dishes may be placed on each set of tables from which children can help themselves if they wish. This method also enables the counter staff to wind up as soon as all the coupons issued for lunch have come in. A table d'hote menu is recommended for school lunchrooms.

College Lunch Rooms

In universities or colleges students do not all have the same lunch hours, and therefore a more leisurely atmosphere prevails in lunchroom. Besides, the students have the choice of eating on the campus or not, and therefore may not be consistent with their eating time or habits. College lunchrooms therefore must provide a mixture of traditional and snaky meals served between fixed hours. The provision of a snack type meal facility helps students to eat when they are in a hurry to reach somewhere and have limited time, besides providing them the means to entertain friends for lunch cheaply. This arrangement also helps managers of lunchrooms to reduce wastage because snack meals can be prepared easily to order, eliminating large volumes of leftovers if the student numbers vary considerably from day-to-day.

School Lunchrooms for the Less Privileged: In government schools particularly at village level, the objective is to provide at least on third of the nutritional requirements through the mid-day meal. The primary function of the school meal in such circumstances becomes that of supplementing the inadequate food intake of the children at home. The reason may be large families and low purchasing power; ignorance of the needs of vulnerable children because of illiteracy of parents; alcoholic male members, who leave little for family meals and so on. As mentioned earlier, the meal may be served anywhere in he school at mid-day. The children are generally made to sit on the floor and served on washed banana or other leaves, which can then be disposed off after the meal. In some schools plastic, aluminum or enamel plates are provided. The foods recommended are a high protein snack, generally a cereal-pulse mixture and a nourishing beverage or seasonal fruit. Peanuts, seeds green vegetables, fruit and milk may be added to the ingredients for the snack to further enhance nutritive value and provide variety. Stuffed paratha (lightly fried layered chappati) and curds provide a good meal. Mid-day meals in these schools ire generally eaten by hand and therefore it is important to inculcate good hygiene practices in the children, be making them wash their hands before and after the meal. Those who dish out the food too should strictly follow these.

Kiosks

Kiosks are structures constructed to provide 4.5 to 5.5 m^2 covered area with one opening for a window or service counter and a door for entrance and exit. The space is provided with one tap for drinking water.

These kiosks may be used as food service outlets and are best suited for the provision of ready to eat snacks and beverages to the public, because of their location on crossroads, near bus stops, etc. Kiosks have been constructed to replace squatters, who used to sell beverages on the roadside. They are usually positioned in every residential area near crossroads, outside offices, schools and community buildings. While kiosks were planned for providing a facility for getting fresh fruit and vegetables on every busy street, people have utilized them in many different ways. It will he seen that with a little imagination the limited space can become a source of attraction to people, or get abandoned due to lack of it.

When using kiosks as food service outlets it is well to remember, that the development authority prohibits cooking on the premises. In spite of this restriction kiosks have developed into a class of food service establishments as popular as the traditional 'dhaba' or roadside cafeteria of old.

The foods recommended for service are ready to eat biscuits, salted snacks, and cookies, boiled eggs, sandwiches to order, fruit and juices. There is space enough for a fruit juice machine, or a small oven in which foods like pizzas, pakoras, and burgers may be reheated on demand. The ideal arrangement would be to place a small microwave oven for heating foods as there is no deterioration in quality with this oven, and it is quick enough to cope with the fast turnover conditions at bus stops, railway platforms, etc. The only deterrent is its high price that if paid, would give good dividends. With one such specialized equipment even a small kiosk can extend its menus, at least seasonally, when prepared foods will keep without refrigeration for a few hours till meal service. One light point is provided in every kiosk but this can be extended with permission, if the owners can afford it. There are twin kiosks also auctioned by the development authority from time to time, for expansion of an establishment. The service methods should be based on the use of disposables to avoid the problem of washing up on the roadsides or in crowded areas. Thus, with an understanding of the characteristics of different foods, and how best they can be utilized for the different needs of people, there is no doubt that any establishment, large or small, will flourish.

Three

Receiving and Storage of Food and Beverages

Once the food materials have been ordered for supply they're handling at the time of delivery represents le process of 'receiving'. A number of precautions are necessary at this stage to ensure that food is not damaged or discarded because of careless handling, spillage, cross contamination and incorrect weights r volumes. It is always beneficial to set up a procedure to be followed by those involved in the receipt of goods. Also, deliveries of various orders come at different times and each-category of food requires separate treatment before it is accepted for storage.

Delivery Methods

There are many ways in which food may be delivered to a food service establishment depending on the nature of the food.

1. Fresh vegetables and fruits may be delivered in jute bags, baskets, cardboard cartons, and wooden chests or as such, depending on the texture, nature and perish ability of the item. For instance, in the case of strawberries or grapes,

cardboard cartons of limited sizes are generally used so that the fruit is not damaged; oranges may be piled in baskets while apples need to be wrapped individually and generally packed in cartons or wooden chests. Vegetables, carrots, lemons, brinjals etc. can be bagged; spinach has to be packed loosely in baskets, and tomatoes in cartons as for fruits. Bulky vegetables like cauliflower, cabbage, jackfruit, etc. are even piled as such in transport vans and delivered.

2. Milk and milk products are generally transported in crates if delivered as pasteurized individual containers. Products like cheese may be bought in blocks wrapped in waterproof packing, so also butter. All milk and milk products are delivered in refrigerated vans especially if bulk supplied and not individually packed. In India, the development of the 'Mother Dairy' is an excellent example of bulk milk transportation and vending.

3. Mates may be delivered as whole carcasses or as different cuts as ordered, depending on the quantities involved. Meal if bought minced, is generally delivered in plastic bags; various proportioned cuts may be in poly packs or disposable trays in which standard portions are packed each covered with a transparent film for easy counting when delivered.

4. Ideally, fish should be delivered in iceboxes or in freezer transport vans to be placed straight in freezer storages especially when ordered and supplied in bulk. This however does not always happen especially in developing countries where the small supplier does not easily afford freezer transportation.

5. Poultry is generally supplied as dressed and drawn birds, on weight basis and packed in cartons or large-sized poly packs delivered in refrigerated vans.

6. Processed food materials that are generally packed in factories are delivered in standard packs of 24's or 48's

or multiples depending on the size of the order. Examples are canned foods, instant powders, spices, biscuits, pasta products, etc.

7. Establishments in gunny or poly packs depending on the quantities required generally buy cereals, flours, pulses and legumes. The jute packs contain 50 to 100 kg, while poly packs vary from 1 to 10 kg.

8. Sugar and salt are delivered in poly packs double packed in cartons.

9. Fats and oils in hermetically sealed containers varying from 1 kg to 15 kg. Oils may be supplied even in drums of 50 or 100 kg from which oil can be siphoned off to issue for use. This method however, is only used in very large establishments.

Delivery Procedure

1. The supplier gets an order in writing stating the date on which supplies are required.

2. He passes it on to his stores department or purchasing officers (depending on the perishability of the food). The order is than kept to be ready for delivery on the specified date.

3. It is transported to the buyer's stores for receiving.

4. The goods are delivered along with two copies of the delivery chalan, one signed by the buyer and returned to the supplier in confirmation of having received the goods; and the second is retained by the buyer for counter checking the bill or invoice when it is received from the supplier for payment.

Receiving Procedure

1. The delivery note is checked with copy of the order placed.

2. Counts, weights or volume are checked to tally with the amounts of various items on the delivery note.

3. The quality of all ingredients is checked with the specifications given to the supplier. Any unacceptable items should be returned with the person bringing the delivery.

4. Any discrepancies noticed should be indicated on the copy of the signed delivery note notified to the supplier. When the delivery note is signed the materials that are delivered have been accepted. In case any damaged item is noticed after the delivery the supplier is informed telephonically. This is followed by a request in writing to replace the same with specified quality, in exchange for the received item.

Receiving materials is generally done close to the storages or just outside them so that it is easier to store them after receipt. In small establishments it may be a matter of providing a receiving bay, that is, a space in which a weighing scale and a worktable is placed to count up or weigh foods as they arrive, and check delivery notes. The area is just outside the main kitchen of the establishment from where most of the fresh ingredients go directly for preparation instead of being stored. In larger establishments the receiving area may be a well designed space provided with weighing, washing and packing facilities for storing food in cold or other storages.

Storage

Storekeeping is one of the most neglected activities in small-scale establishments. The first principle in storekeeping is to know 'what' is 'where' when the user department needs it.

Most food materials need to be stored for different lengths of time and at different temperatures, to reserve their wholesomeness till required for preparation and service. For effective storage of food items therefore, two types of storages are used the dry storage rooms meant for non-perishable commodities like cereals and their products, pulses, legumes, sugar and spices, canned foods, fats and oils, etc. and the low temperature storages for semi-perishable and perishable foods.

Food stores in all establishments should be situated for easy access by staff of user departments as well as suppliers, without interference in the flow of work of, all concerned.

Dry storerooms should be well lighted so that every item placed in them is easily visible and identifiable. Good ventilation helps to prevent spoilage, and maintain the temperatures required. From the point of view of security, it is general practice to provide only one entrance-exit to stores. This also provides better control of deliveries and issues to user departments.

It would suffice here, to mention that storage equipment is now designed for easy reach and mobility, so that even small establishments can get storerooms cleaned without having to completely empty them. A lot of damage is done to quality where foods are not stored in a systematic manner.

Organization of Storages

The arrangement of food items in storage spaces affects the efficiency with which foods can be stocked, issued and re-ordered. Any system adopted therefore, should aim at establishing a flow of material in and out of the stores in a manner that will preserve the qualities of foods to the maximum. Haphazard arrangements lead to situations where fresh stocks may be issued before earlier ones are used up; or more orders for an item placed because none of it could be easily located on the shelves when required.

The following suggestions will prove helpful in creating a systematic arrangement of food items in storage.

(i)   Arrange food according to the type of commodity.
(ii) Place stock items in alphabetical order of food categories.

(iii) Stamp the date of delivery on every stock received before shelving to ensure that old stocks are used up first,

(iv) Place items on shelves according to date stamped, with earlier ones in the front of a row, and later ones at the back. Stamping also helps to cost the stocks more accurately according to the prices paid on the bill for the particular lot.

(v) Mark prices on stocks as well. The information can then be made readily available to the user department and helps a catering manager to calculate the food costs and hence the selling prices of prepared dishes more realistically.

(vi) Arrange products to give an organized appearance. Efforts should be made to ensure that commodities do not lie around on the floor at any time. Heavy bins or drums should also be placed on wheels or on a slatted platform, for free circulation of air around the food packs.

Alphabetic Arrangement of Items in Stocks

Cereals	Canned fruit	Nuts	Spices
Bajra	Apples	Almonds	Chilies
Barley	Apricots	Cashew nuts	Coriander
Jowar	Berries	Peanut	Cumin
Maize	Cherries	Pistachio	Fenugreek
Oatmeal	Dates	Walnuts	Pepper
Rice	Figs		Turmeric

General Procedure for Storage

Jute or Poly Bags

All items delivered in bulk bags like sugar, flour, cereals, pulses, etc. should be cross stacked keeping a maximum of six bags to a stack, which is placed on a slatted platform. Any opened bags should be immediately emptied into metal or plastic bins, polyethylene drums or cans with tight fitting lids.

Cross-stacking helps free air circulation. Poly bags of milk powder should preferably be refrigerated. This would require much space and therefore only large establishments that would buy milk powder in bulk and have refrigerated rooms for milk and milk products, eggs, and other perishable foods would be able to store it.

Cartons and Cases

Canons of canned foods, biscuits, etc. should be stacked with their labels visible 'or identification, and open on the side for easy access to packs.

Tins or Small Cardboard Packs or Jars

These packs are generally used for dried fruits, preserves, mixes, jellies, etc. and may be lined up one in front of the other, each row having packs of the same item. This helps in having the first horizontal rows representing all different items of food in stock, easy to locate for issue when required.

As a rule vegetables and fruits require to be stored in areas separate from the main dry stores, especially root vegetables. This is because root vegetables pass on their odours to other foods easily, and through respiration also increase the temperature of the stove. Oils and fats need special attention in storage because they tend to get rancid in the presence of light. They also absorb odours and flavours from other foods. Knowledge of foods that easily absorb or give off strong odours is necessary to help keep foods in storage from being adversely affected.

Low temperature storages are based on the fact that microbial activity decreases with decrease in temperature, and thereby prolongs the storage life of perishable items. Eggs and dairy products require temperatures of 5-10°C as against meat, fish and poultry which need to be stored at 0 to20°C, if stored for more than two or three days. For a short period of 2-3 days 0-3°C is sufficient.

Storekeeping

Maintaining stores efficiently requires a good communication system between the storekeeper and the user departments, to know their needs specifically. Training and experience are necessary for accurate record keeping and negotiating with the suppliers. Above all, every storekeeper must have a high standard of ethics because he is in a very vulnerable position, handling stores of value that every man requires and would like to have. He is also vulnerable to getting corrupted by sellers and staff alike.

Store Records

A number of records need to be maintained as foods move very fast in and out of the stores, and it is necessary to be able to account for them at any time.

Requisition Slip: This is a request form submitted by user departments to the stores in charge for the issue of required items. Depending on the size of the establishment and the number of user department's different coloured slips may be used for each department.

Sample of a Requisition Slip

Department		Date
Food Item	Unit	Amount Required
		Signature of Requisitioning Authority

It is customary to put in requisition slips to the stores at least one day in advance, so that the food items required for the next day are collected and issued in time for food preparation. In large establishments, a separate transit store exists, from which items required daily are used up. When the levels in this store or kitchen cupboard go down, then a fresh requisition slip is issued to the main store to mark up the levels.

Order Form

A person authorized to do so must sign an order. Generally, the catering manager authorizes purchase in a small establishment, and a purchasing manager in an establishment that has a purchasing department. Three copies of an order are prepared, one each for supplier, ordering department and stores in charge that would receive the goods when they arrive.

Order

From: To:	Ref No.: Date:

Please supply the following items by Date

Item   Quantity   Unit   Value

Manager

Once the order has been executed, the items received are entered in a 'goods received" book as shown below:

Goods Received Book

Date	Item Description	Unit	Quantity	Order No.	Supplier
1.					
2.					
3.					
4.					

Stock Book

In this, records of all items received and issued are maintained along with stocks in hand and their monetary value. This enables a storekeeper to see at a glance, the quantities of any particular item in stock at any time. It thus helps him to place orders before stocks are completely depleted.

Invoice

This is the bill that follows a delivery, to be paid for by the buyer. In food service establishments the storekeeper to the accounts section for payment usually sends the invoice, after verification of items and rates.

Maintenance of Food Quality in Storage

Where large quantities of food materials are stored, it is imperative that steps be taken to ensure that the quality of foods does not deteriorate on storage.

(a) *Excessive handling*: This can damage packages, making it possible for foods like biscuits, noodles or other cereal products to become soggy or moldy or broken making then unfit for serving.

(b) *Temperature and humidity*: Uncontrolled temperatures and humidity can lead to evaporation or absorption of moisture, leading to drying or sogginess the latter providing suitable conditions for microbial growth.

(c) *Damage*: Damage to food like fruits and vegetables can cause enzymatic and oxidative discolouration affecting their quality.

(d) Sunlight in stores at certain times of the day, falling on milk and milk products, or other vitamin B_2 containing foods can affect the content of this vitamin.

(e) Infestation of cereals and pulses by weevils, presence of white ants in the store, or rodents and other pests can damage the flavour, and quality of foods, making them unfit for consumption.

Sample of Stock Book

Item				Price	
Unit				Max. Stock Level	
				Min. Stock Level	
Date of Stock	Stock Level	Received	Issued	Balance Stock	Value

With all these factors in mind, efforts should be aimed at increasing shelf life of foods through care in receiving and storage, while at the same time maintaining quality.

Receiving of Beverages

The objectives for beverage receiving are similar in many ways to those of receiving. However as the value of beverage purchases and the ensuing profits from the sale of beverages are high, it is important that due attention is given to the receiving of beverages

The main objectives are:

1. The quantity of beverages delivered matches that which has been ordered. This requires a methodical approach to checking the goods against the purchase order and the delivery note. Items would be in standard units of crates, cases etc. with standard contents of a specific size. Crates and cases should be opened to check for such things as empty, missing or broken bottles.

2. The quality inspection is simple, but again requires a thorough and methodical approach. It involves such things as checking the brand name and label on each item, the alcohol proof, the vintage and shipper, against the delivery note and the purchase order.

3. The prices stated on the delivery note are in accordance with the negotiated prices shown on the purchase order form.

4. When the quantity or quality of the beverage delivered is not in accordance with the purchase order or an item is omitted from the order that the receiving clerk or cellarman raises a request for credit note.

5. An accurate record is kept of all goods received book recording details of the delivery.

6. An accurate record is kept of all chargeable empties delivered and returned.

7. Deliveries of beverages are timetabled with the suppliers often to an afternoon, when receiving and cellar staff are normally not so busy and the receiving area is free from other deliveries.

Storing and Issuing of Beverages

Once beverages are received it must be removed immediately to the cellar and a tight level of control maintained at all times. The storage of beverages is ideally separated into five areas as:

(a) The main storage area for spirits and red wine held at a dry and draught free temperature of 13-16°. This area is also used for the general collection and preparation of orders for the various bars and the storage of beverage when there is a reasonable turnover.

(b) A refrigerated area of 10° for the storage of white and sparkling wines.

(c) A further refrigerated area of 6-8°. This is really necessary only when the turnover is slow.

(d) An area held at a temperature of 13° for the storage of bottle beers and soft drinks

(e) A totally separate area from the above for the storage of empty bottles and crates

This area needs to be as tightly controlled as the beverage storage area not only because of the returnable value of the crates and bottles, but to prevent access by bar staff when an empty for full bottle method of issuing is in operation.

The merchandise is unpacked in the cellar and stored correctly on shelves or racks in the same order as on the standard bottle code/bin list. The objective for preparing a standard bottle code/bin list is to eliminate the confusion of bottle sizes, spelling of names and different brands and to establish an appropriate starting point for the control of beverages. All requisitions, inventories, wine list are related to the code/bin list.

Cellar Records

As the value of cellar stocks is high, it is usual for the following cellar records to be kept.

Cellar Inwards Book

This provides accurate reference to all beverages coming into the cellar and posting data for the cellarman's bin cards. Whenever necessary it is a useful check against the perpetual beverage inventory ledger held in the food and beverage control or account office.

Bin Cards

These are provided for each individual type of beverage held in stock and record all deliveries and issues made the cards being fixed on the shelves or racks against each beverage, the bin card numbers referring to the same bin numbers as the wine list and originating from the standard code list.

Cellar Control Book

This provides a record of all daily deliveries to the cellar and the daily issues of each beverage from the cellar to the various bars and should crosscheck with the entries on the bin cards and the perpetual inventory ledger held in the food control or the account office.

Beverages Perpetual Inventory Ledger

This master ledger, which is prepared in the control or account office, consists of cards prepared for each individual type of beverage held in stock. The purpose is to keep a daily record of any purchases of the separate types of beverages and of the quantities issued from the cellar to each individual bar or other area and to record a perpetual inventory balance for each item. The information is obtained from the supplier's delivery notes or invoices and the daily beverages requisition notes from the different bars. When the physical stocktaking of the cellar is undertaken, the physical stocktaking figures should match to those in the perpetual inventory ledger.

Breakages

It is necessary for breakages to be recorded on a standard form, together with an explanation and countersigned by a member of the food and beverages management department. The frequency of any breakage would determine the necessity for management to take corrective action. Breakages of bottled beverages usually occur by mishandling by cellar and bar staff.

Empties Return Book

The supplier against a delivery charges many of the containers of beverages such as crates, beer bottles, soda siphons, etc. for. It is therefore necessary that control be maintained on these charged items to ensure that they are returned to the supplier and the correct credit obtained. A container record book is required which records all containers returned and the balance matching the stocktaking of containers.

Hospitality Book

This is necessary to record the issue of drinks to the kitchen and other grades of staff as laid down by the company policy.

Issuing of Beverages

Issuing of beverages should take place at set times during the day and only against a requisition note signed by an authorized person for example head barman banqueting head waiter, etc. Ideally when the requisition is a large one it should be handed in several hours before the items are required to allow the cellar staff plenty of time to assemble the order together. Requisition notes are usually made in duplicate, one copy being retained by the cellarman so that entries can be made to the cellar records and then it is passed to the control or accounts office, while the second copy is retained by the person who originated the requisition and handed in with the daily taking and other control documents.

The pricing of issues for beverages is different from that for food in that two prices are recorded the cost price and the selling price. The cost price is recorded to credit the cellar account and for trading account and balance sheet purposes.

The selling price is recorded for control purposes to measure the sales potential of a selling outlet using the basic formula:

Opening stock + purchases – closing stock = total beverage cosumed
Total beverage consumed = beveragerevenue

It should be noted that the above formula might be calculated for the value of stock and purchases either.

At cost price in order to compare the usage with the actual sales and to ascertain the profit margin and beverages gross profit.

At sales price in order to compare potential sales with the actual recorded sales.

It is usual for the beverages revenue to be different for sales potential figure because of such factors as a high percentage of mixed drinks being sold or full bottle sales being made over the counter of a bar.

Stocktaking of Beverages

The main objectives of stocktaking are

1. To determine the total value of all beverages held in stock. This will indicate if too much is held in stock and if it is in line with the financial and catering policies.
2. To compare the actual value of beverages held in the cellar at a specific time with the book value of the stock, which will have been calculated with the simple formula:

   Value of opening stock + purchases during period – requisitions during the same periods = value of closing stock

3. To identify slow moving items.
4. To compare beverage usage at cost with beverage gross profit.
5. To check security and control system.
6. To determine the rate of stock turnover.

The value and volume of the closing stock are also checked against the information from the perpetual inventory ledger cards for each beverage. The stocktaking should highlight any differences and indicate the efficiency of the cellar staff and the beverage control system.

The stocktaking should be undertaken by staff from the control or accounts department together with members of the food and beverage management team. As is the case with food stocktaking it is necessary that this be done at the end of every trading period and before if possible the beginning of the next period. This requires staff to work late at night or early in the morning and at times at the weekends.

Four

Menu Planning

A menu is virtually a list, of dishes planned for production in-a catering operation and many include full meals snacks or beverages. It performs a number of functions:

1. Introduces the establishment to the customer.
2. Authorizes production of meals in the kitchen.
3. Helps to prepare shopping list for foods and ingredients and are the basis for establishing purchasing procedures.
4. Determines the type of equipment, staff skills and the type of supervision required.
5. Helps to organize spaces and work in stores, kitchens and service areas.
6. Determines the style of service to be set up.
7. Forms the basis for the calculation of food and labour costs, overhead expenses and desired profits.
8. Reflects the type of customer the establishment wishes to attract.
9. Satisfies the needs of the customers for nutrition, hunger, as well as social and psychological needs.
10. Introduces interesting food combinations to customers,

and through specialty foods impart knowledge of the foods eaten in different states, countries and cultures.

11. Provides a means of developing good eating habits in people.

There is no doubt from the above that the menu forms the core of all other activities in a food service establishment.

The success of a food service operation, no matter what its size, depends heavily on those who plan the menus and how they do it. While it may seem a simple exercise of providing something to eat and drink, in practice good menu planning requires a lot of skill. It is important therefore, that people responsible for planning menus have the following qualifications:

Wide Knowledge of Foods

This involves knowledge about different kinds and varieties of foods; their seasonal availability; nutritional and anti-nutritional factors; and the presence of toxic elements in certain food varieties; the edible portion obtained from each food; colour, taste and flavour differences and how they can best be combined for meals; acceptability; and cost factors.

Knowledge of Different Methods of Preparing and Serving Foods

Even though the menu planner does not necessarily prepare or serve the food, it is important for him to know which food is best prepared by which method of cooking. This is possible only if the planner knows about the inherent qualities of foods in terms of texture, composition, colour, flavour, and all other chemical and physical properties. The knowledge of the behaviour of these characteristics to the application of heat, addition of salts, acids, oils and spices, so essential to any method of food preparation, is also important.

Similarly, knowing what food is suited to what style of service;

which flavours Wend together best, and how to combine them, are the crux of a customer's acceptability of the food.

Knowledge of the Ways in Which Food can be Aesthetically Presented

Whatever may be the colour, taste and flavour of a meal, its appearance on the plate or in the display case determines customer's choice. Equipped with this knowledge the menu planner can introduce a variety of form and colour in menus to attract the customers.

Knowledge of the Customer

It is vital for the menu planner to be familiar with the food expectations if the customer. A general idea of his food preferences or favourites, physiological requirements, paying power, social standing, and the reasons for eating out are essential for achieving customer satisfaction.

People eat outside their homes for a number of different reasons, and each one affects their choice of food at a particular time. For instance, office goers stopping for a quick lunch would prefer light inexpensive meals, while an executive who is entertaining would choose more elaborately presented items, Similarly, captive customers, such as children in a boarding school, or people in an old age home will necessarily eat from a less selective menu, because they have no choice but to eat what is prepared in the institutional kitchen. Again, people traveling long distances look forward to food, because other activities r movements on a train or an aeroplane are restricted. The menus should therefore be interesting in terms of providing variety in form, colour and flavour. In addition, they need to be easy to serve and eat while traveling.

Also, people have very strong likes and dislikes because of cultural, religious or traditional reasons. For instance, in India people have taboos regarding the eating of beef; most people are vegetarians, and some religious orders do not permit even the consumption of onions and garlic. While it is not possible to provide for each and every customer's needs, menu planning that shows in consideration for these special needs is to be commended. It is a challenge therefore, to the planner to provide variety and interest in a meal according to the general needs and expectations of the customer.

To do this, the planner does not only have to be knowledgeable but also imaginative and creative.

In a catering establishment the person who plans the meals is also generally required to perform the tasks of ordering foodstuffs from suppliers; liaising with stores for issue of non-perishables; preparing kitchen schedules and staff rotors; supervising service, etc. The number and nature of the tasks vary with the size and type of establishment.

Planning menus becomes essential when food has to be bought, prepared and served in large quantities to people of varying tastes and requirements. The advantages gained from planning are:

(a) An ability to provide appetizing, nourishing and attractive meals to customers at a fair price. This is only possible if the meals are planned in advance, so that a price advantage can be obtained by buying seasonal foods and in quantities that carry discounts.

(b) Planning meals helps to determine requirements accurately. Food buying can thus be controlled through advance buying, because quantities are calculated beforehand.

(c) Planning ensures that food is not wasted because any leftovers can be creatively incorporated in the next day's menu that is already planned out.

(d) Time and effort spent on haphazard ordering, shopping and receiving of food materials is saved to a large extent.

(e) Time and effort spent in preparation and cooking is also minimized because ingredients needed for subsequent meals are known in advance. For instance, garnishes can be prepared along with salads at one time. Chopping and cutting separately for each dish is avoided. Time is not lost in waiting for ingredients, as they are already purchased and ready for use.

(f) Carefully planned menus save fuel and cut down on waste through excessive leftovers. For example, milk may be heated together for the preparation of hot beverages, setting of curds, or for preparing cottage cheese, instead of placing the milk in three containers and heating small quantities separately. Similarly, planned menus can help to save on quantities and ingredients, e.g. leftover curds may be added to boiling milk for making cottage cheese or 'paneer' instead of vinegar or lemon juice. Also, the whey obtained need not be wasted, but added to curries, soups, etc.

(g) Planned menus help to note favourite dishes and those that did not sell too well in the past. From these records, decisions regarding the number of portions of each item to be prepared for service can be made,

(h) Planned menus also tend to offer a wider choice of dishes because seasonal varieties of foods can be introduced in advance. This becomes very restricted when preparation has to be done on the basis of spot decisions.

(i) Advance planning removes a lot of anxiety for the planner, and enables clear-cut instructions to be given to staff. This also helps to create harmony among people at work.

(j) If the planner cannot come to work one day, the customer does not have to go hungry or disappointed, because the work goes on according to plan.

(k) Meal planning helps in the accurate calculation of food costs and inclusion of items that can be profitably sold. It also becomes far easier to fix selling prices in advance for the information of the customer.

(l) Planning helps to take care of price fluctuations so that there are no frequent changes on menu displays as far as the customer is concerned.

Planning menus is thus an important activity for every food service operation and catering managers need to ensure procedures, which can determine how best it can be done.

Planning Menus

Before actually writing down the items on the menu, every planner must consider the basic factors important to the situation and the customer for whom the menu is being planned.

Situations

The basic factors to be considered in terms of the situation would be:

(a) Location of the establishment in relation to the market.
(b) Space available for storing food in wholesome condition.
(c) Size of kitchen and service areas.
(d) Number of staff and their skills.
(e) Equipment available in kitchen and service areas.
(f) Policy of the establishment in terms of:
  (i) What type of customers it wishes to attract. This will be basically determined by the pricing policy, in that the higher the prices, the richer the customer and the higher his power to pay.
  (ii) The extent to which the establishment wishes to invest on catering, in comparison to other areas of expenditure like furniture, decor, equipment, and so on.
  (iii) Degree of automation or labour-saving devices desired,
  (iv) Personnel in terms of trained staff or cheaper unskilled labour,

    (v) Profit margins.

    (vi) Type of service, i.e. whether food is served or plated and handed over or packed and delivered.

Customer

Customers are likely to represent people of varying ages, activities, occupations, physiological status and sex. They would also belong to various religious and cultural backgrounds, some perhaps, having rigid food habits. The following discussion will illustrate how the various requirements of customers form the basis for menu planning.

If a menu has to be planned for school children living in a boarding school, the factors to consider would be:

(a) School children generally spend a lot of physical energy at play. They are also at various stages of growth and so their general nutritional needs would have to be considered while planning their meals. Some children may have special requirements because of sickness or injury. The considerations would therefore place emphasis on planning balanced diets suitable to their need.

(b) Children are generally restless and do not like to spend too much time at the table eating. Besides, they feel rushed in the morning because they must reach their class on time. So menus have to provide dishes that are quick to eat, and yet satisfying. Perhaps something they can carry out of the dining hall without messing themselves, such as a hamburger or a salad roll; or stuffed parathas, pancakes, and whole fruit would be in order.

(c) Children also tend to get bored with foods easily. So menus need to provide variety in colour, texture, taste and flavor.

(d) The climatic and weather conditions are an important consideration too. In very dry and hot weather, children lose a lot of body water and salts through perspiration.

The menus then would need to introduce extra liquids and salts, because children do not generally like to drink plain water.

In humid hot climates the feeling is that of stress, lethargy and discomfort, and spirits sag. In such conditions, meals need to provide cool, foods like ices, chilled juices and fruits, cold meats, crisp salads, cold soups and other refreshing and nourishing drinks.

In cold climates, on the other hand, extra energy is required to keep warm, and fried crisp foods like croquettes, cutlets, chips, kebabs, samosas or fried rice, pulaos, hot breads and hot beverages and desserts would be the choices,

(e) Children have varying appetites and often prefer snaky meals at frequent intervals, to a few large ones.

(f) In general, boys prefer foods with a higher satiety and caloric value than girls of the same age, who become figure conscious and prefer light, frequent but small meals. Also, girls generally prefer foods that are more highly spiced.

The menu planner therefore, has to consider all these factors when planning menus for children, in addition to making them cost effective, tempting and profitable. Below are some sample menus for different types of customers indicating the special features considered in planning.

Menu A: A day's menu for a boy's boarding school

Break Fast	Lunch	Tea	Dinner
Egg	Curry	Samosa	Spinach Dal
Buttered toast	Sauteed vegetable	Milk shake	Sauteed potatoes
Milk	Curd (yoghurt)		Chappati
Fruit	Chappati, Roti		Rice
	Rice		Sweet Dish Halwa

The menu pattern has taken into consideration the following factors:

(a) The Indian food habits that include a curry, curd, dal preparation (usually consumed in some form at least once a day), an Indian dessert at dinner.

(b) Boys need nutritional balance provided by foods from all food groups in each meal. Satiety value through a fried snack, egg and Sweet dish (halwa) take care of protein and extra calories for activities.

(c) The menu provides in its formal, a lot of flexibility, so that different curries, halwas, forms of egg, snacks, fruits and shakes can be provided according to seasonal availability.

(d) It may be noted that boys do not like salads unless they are incorporated in sandwiches or rolls, which can be introduced as snacks.

Menu B: A day's menu for a girl's hostel

Breakfast	Lunch	Tea	Dinner
Porridge	Curry	Pakoras	Dal
Egg (Poached)	Raita	Chutney	Sauteed vegetable
Buttered toast	Salad	Tea	Chappati
Milk	Chappati, Roti		Rice
Fruit	Pickle		Sweet Dish Halwa/Kheer

The difference in Menus A and B is chiefly in the provision of spicy preparations like 'raitas', pickle and assorted pakoras. Also salads and egg have been provided in preference to fried forms. The menu is just as flexible and can be varied according to the mood of the customer and the availability of ingredients.

It may be noted that Menus A and B are only samples, and if a cyclic menu is prepared which is the normal practice in hostels, then specific dishes may be written out for several days in advance.

Menu C: Conference lunch menu attended by delegates from different countries

1.	Stiffed Capsicum and Tomatoes
2.	Cottage cheese/Meat ball curry
3.	Mixed vegetables pulao
4.	Pineapple raita
5.	Green salad
6.	Carrot halawa mould with ream
7.	Coffee

The factors taken into consideration are:

(a) The dishes planned are generally acceptable to persons from all countries. The menu accomplishes this because the starter and salad are two items that are eaten all over the world. The curry selected is familiar to most persons as meatballs served with spaghetti or in tomato sauce are common to most. Cottage cheese curry provides vegetarians with an equivalent substitute for meat curry. People from all countries relish Indian curries. Rice is a common cereal in most countries and people look forward to tasting oriental flavours in the form of 'pulaos'. Pineapple raita would provide the familiar flavour of fruit yoghurt while acting as a suitable accompaniment to the rice. Carrot halwa moulded and served with cream introduces a new form of pudding to foreign palates, while being relished by most Indians.

(b) The composition of the menu allows for quick service between conference sessions.

(c) Colour, texture, flavour and attractiveness is taken care of through providing different heights on a buffet table during service.

(d) There is very little scope for over spicing. For those who wish to add more spices, these could be placed on the table.

Menu D: Canteen Menu

Special for the day Assorted fried snack Sandwiches Fruit Cake Tea	Pizza

Factors considered in planning are:

(a) Habits of the customers for instance, if it is an office canteen, hot beverages will be demanded all day.
(b) Purchasing power of the customer.
(c) Favourites among customers especially included in the days special.
(d) Easy to serve in disposables.
(e) Satiety value and value for money.
(f) Minimum on the spot preparation.
(g) Items that will provide attractive displays.

The above menus provide only an insight into the art of menu planning for particular situations. No amount of descriptions or illustrations can replace the results of the actual experiences of menu planners with their particular situations and customer. Each category requires initiative, creativity and imagination with consideration for physical, psychological and social requirements.

The objectives of a good menu plan meeting nutritional requirements of school children (Menus A and B) can be completely marred if children from the boarding school go out and eat in a cafe or canteen. As seen from Menu D, canteens need not always focus attention on nutritional value. This is because even if they did, children may not make the right choices in buying.

While menu planning has its advantages, it also requires a lot of time and thought to be effective. The effort of every planner, therefore, should be to minimize the time spent on other activities.

In order to do this it is a good policy to plan meals several days ahead, as this helps to:

(i) Prepare market orders in advance and reduce last minute purchasing. It also allows enough time to shop when markets are least crowded.

(ii) Helps to control costs through cheaper buying when larger amounts are needed for a week's supply as against daily shopping.

With practice and experience, menu planning too can become a less and less time consuming, and more:

Writing Menus

1. Use a pencil to write menus so that it is easier to erase an item if changed, till the plan is finalized.

2. Keep handy:

(a) An indexed updated file of standard recipes giving costs, portions, selling price per portion, gross profit percentage along with ingredients and methods. It will help to include the name of alternate cost equivalent ingredients for use in the recipe in case of lack of availability of some ingredient. An index number for cross-reference is necessary for locating and consulting other pages in the file.

(b) Lists of prices of seasonal and other foods, updated for ready reference.

(c) Lists of substitute foods in the form of exchange list.

(d) Ideas for use of leftovers, developed with experience.

(e) List of the most profitable dishes.

(f) Lists of foods in stock at the time of planning in terms of leftovers, prepared and raw foods. It is useful to have stock lists in order, that will enable earlier stocks to be planned into menus first before fresh ones are used,

    (g) List of staff on leave so that skills of existing staff can be kept in mind before placing an item on the menu.

    (h) Lists of popular food combinations.

3. With the above available aids and the basic considerations in mind, menus can be written out with names of dishes in the following order:

    (a) Starter/soup,

    (b) Main dish

    (c) Side dish/(es)

    (d) Cereal preparation

    (e) Salad

    (f) Accompaniments

    (g) Dessert

    (h) Hot beverage

The sample menu A and B in table indicates order with the dishes as planned.

A	B
Egg drop tomato soup	Grilled stuffed tomatoes
Tandoori chicken	Baked fish/cheese
Paneer/kofta curry	Sauted peas and corn
Meat or vegetable balls	Sunshine salad
Pulao/fried rice	Garlic bread
Naan/Roti	Steamed chocolate pudding
Onion tomato salad	
Sweet dish	Coffee

4. Menus must be written in a form that is simple, legible and attractive to draw the customer's attention.

5. Names of dishes should be clearly understood. If unfamiliar names are used, description should follow the names so that the customer knows exactly what he is ordering.

6. Sauces and accompaniments create a feeling of getting good value for money', and must be indicated on the menu. These may be written as a separate item, or along with the dish for which it is the special accompaniment.

7. Care is necessary in word selection and correct spelling of dishes, particularly if they are written in a foreign language. For example 'Half-Fried Chicken' will convey a different meaning to the customer than 'Fried Half Chicken'.

8. Portion sizes must be indicated along with prices (Menu D) so that the customer does not feel cheated. In some cafeterias the price is expected to indicate the portion size, but this is sometimes deceptive and damages consumer relations.

Menus can be written in many different ways according to the purpose for which they are intended. In food services where a waiter style of service is offered, the menu is generally presented in the form of a folder. This introduces the establishment to the customer and therefore gives information other than the list of dishes and prices. It covers the address, telephone numbers, service timing and other relevant information.

In a canteen, lunchroom or cafeteria, the menu would probably be displayed as a list of items with prices on a board. In smaller establishments a blackboard and chalk may be used to write the date and menu items offered every day.

On formal occasions small menu cards may be placed in front of each guest cover for letting guests know in which order items will be served. Such menus generally indicate the set menu ordered by the host. Each card also carries the guest name on it so that each guest is directed to his proper position at the table vis-a-vis the host/hostess.

In institutions like hostels, hospitals, homes, menus are charted out for a week or ten days in advance, according to a meal plan varying from a three to five meals a day routine. This plan would include breakfast, lunch and dinner, with some institutions providing something at tea and/or bedtime also. Some establishments may even provide a beverage, fruit or midmorning snack.

In institutional menus, it is not the practice to indicate prices or portions because these establishments are generally non-profit making, and the customers or inmates at the point of service never pay the price for meals.

The decoration and colour used on menu cards should blend with the general decor and nature of the establishment. It should be attractive and pleasing, and not detract from the items listed.

Types of Menus

Menus are basically of three types:

(a) A la Carte;
(b) Table d'hote; and
(c) A combination of the two.

A la Carte Menu

This menu is basically a choice menu and generally offers choices of dishes or items to customers under ten food categories.

The categories in an a la carte menu generally follow a sequence on the menu card, in which the customer would normally select items for the meal. Each dish is priced separately so that a choice can be made according to the taste and purchasing power of the customer.

A la carte menus may range from being limited to a few items in a coffee shop, canteen or cafeteria to being extensive in the case of restaurants providing waiter service. These menus are used chiefly by profit-making establishments, and are suitable for leisurely dining, because the wide choices offered and selected, take longer to process in the kitchen before they can be served

The advantage of a la carte menu is that customers can choose any item according to their appetite, mood and pocket.

Starters	Soups	Main Dishe	Side Dishes	Cereal Preparations
Jal Jeera	Rasam	Fish	Vegetable cooked	Chapati
Egg	Mushroom	Chicken	in various ways	Paratha
Prawn	Tomato	Mutton		Naan
Cocktail				
Assorted Snack				
Assorted Salads	Chicken	Cottage Cheese		Rice Preparation
Stuffed Tomato	Goulash	Stews		Breads
Spring rolls	French	Legumes		Puris
	Onion			

Salad	Desserts	Sandwiches	Snacks	Beverages
Tomato onion	Fruits	Ribbon	Fried	Tea
Spring salad	Ice cream	Chutney	Sandwiches	Coffee
Green salad	Soufflés	Salad	Grilled	Buttermilk
Beetroot radish	Pies	Chicken	Baked	Hot chocolate
Salad				
Russian salad	Custard Double	Decker	Milk shakes	
Waldorf salad		Club		Juices
Mixed tossed		Scandinavian		
Salad				

Table d'Hote Menu

Table d'hote means 'table of the host'. This menu is therefore a set menu, in which a number of dishes are planned by the host and food served and offered at a set price. Some establishments especially those located in out of the way places with seasonal customers, such as at hill stations in tropical countries or at places of pilgrimage where worshippers flock together at certain limes of the year, follow set menus. Their selling policy is a 'lake-it-or-leave-it' one, and little or no flexibility is built into the table d'hote menus. This is so even when catering for travelers as on railways, airlines, etc. A typical table d'hote menu is served in India in the form of 'thali' meals in some establishments and on trains. In the latter, stainless steel trays with sections of various sizes for serving the different menu items, are generally used. Similarly, the 'tray' meals served on an aircraft is all set menus. Gradually table d'hote menus too are increasingly being planned to provide a little flexibility in the form of at least a choice of soup or beverage.

Club Menu	Railway Menu
Dinner	**Dinner Tray**
Mushroom soup	Non-vegetarian
Roast Potato	Mutton/Chiken curry
Roast Mutton,	Sautee Potatoes
Mint Sauce	Spinach
Butter cabbage	Curd
Vegetable cutlet	Salad
Indian Vegetarian Dinner	**Rice boiloed**
Mushroom soup	Chappati
Lauki Masala	Papad
Mutter Mushroom Curry	Pickle
Dal Urad	
Tandoori Roti	Vegetarian Tray
Caramel Custard	Dal/Kofta Curry
	Sauted Potato Spinach
	(Rest is same as above)
College Canteen Menu	Airline Menu
Vegetable Burger	Chicken/Cheese Pattie
Chicken Chowmien	Salad with French
Samosa with chutney	Dressing
Idli with sambhar	Pulao
Cake	Cream cake or Lemon
Tea	Tart
Coffee	
Cold Drinks	

Combination Menu

In some establishments it is common to have a la carte menus with a 'Special for the Day' attachment to it. This 'special' may be a set of dishes with an accompaniment, or a plated meal offered in a table d'hote form at a set price. More and more establishments are now including vegetarian and Chinese dishes on their menus for the odd customer.

Food service establishments should be able to provide at any time, an alternative to the planned menus, if customers' food habits demand, keeping ethnic preferences in mind, For example, if a customer does lot eat eggs, the food service should be able to make an omelettfi without it. Alternatives could be 'besan poora' in which the egg is substituted by gram flour and a batter prepared, spread thinly on a hot griddle, cooked, folded like an omelette and served.

Use of Menus

Menus may be used in a number of ways according to the requirements of food service establishments, since menu planning is a time and effort consuming activity, it is not advisable to change menu plans too frequently. A la carte menus are hardly ever changed since they provide a large choice for the customer anyway. The only reasons for change would be increase in cost prices of dishes which may make some dishes unprofitable to serve; change in tastes of customers who do not demand the dish any longer; or retirement or resignation of the specialist cook preparing the dish. Table d' hole menus are changed more frequently to provide variety of set menus within the same price range.

Cyclic Menu

In the case of hotels, hospitals, homes and other institutions, menus are planned in advance for periods of time varying from five days to one month. These are then cycled or repeated. Such menus are termed as 'cyclic' menus and are usually combination type menus providing choices within a set framework.

Menus are generally used cyclically in establishments with captive consumers, whose numbers do not vary appreciably and where tight budget limits prevail. Also the special requirements of these customers re known over a period of time and can be incorporated into the menu as required.

With short-term cycles, however, there is a tendency to produce menu fatigue. The customers tend to remember what is served on Mondays, for example, and may look forward to meal only on a favourite menu day.

To counteract this a number of methods are adopted:

(a) Planning is done for an odd number of days, so that the same menu does not fall on the same day of the week, or same date of a month. For example, plans may be made for 5, 10 or 20 days to prevent people associating a particular menu with a particular day of the week.

(b) A general menu structure may be set, but dishes changed to introduce variety. For example, a menu may say 'seasonal vegetable' or 'curried meat' so that the customer does not really know what he is getting. It could be peas on one day, cauliflower on another, and meat curry followed by curried mince or meat balls, and so on. Variations can also be introduced through different methods of cooking the same food. This also provides flexibility to the planner, who can with confidence mix and match foods and flavours according to stocks, availability, budget and special occasions, etc.

Cyclic Menu

Meal	Monday	Tuesday	Wednesday	Thursday	Friday	Saturday	Sunday
Breakfast	Porridage,	Idli, chutney	Egg.	Uppama	Egg on toast	Porridage	Paratha
	Butter, jam	Milk/Tea	Bread butter	Fruit, milk	Tea/Coffee	Milk	Curd
	Milk/Tea	Coffee	Milk/Tea	Tea/Coffee	Fruit	Tea/Coffee	Tea
	Coffee	Fruit	Coffee				Coffee
Lunch	Curry, salad	Curry	Curry, Raita	Curry Seasonal	Curry curd	Curry	Biryani
	Papad/Pickle	Seasonal	Fried Rice	Vegetable	Pulao	Seasonal	Salad
	Rice	Vegetable	Roti	Salad Roti	Roti	Vegetable	Raita
	Roti	Salad Rice	Pickle	Rice	Salad	Salad	Pickle
		Roti				Rice/Roti	
Tea	Sandwiches	Biscuits	Samosa	Cake	Cutlets	Pakora	Burger
	Tea	Tea	Tea	Tea	Tea	Tea	Tea
Dinner	Dal	Dal seasonal	Soup pasta	Dal seasonal	Soup	Dal	Soup
	Seasonal	Vegetables	Preparation	Vegetables	Pizza	Seasonal	Cutlets
	Vegetables	Salad	Stewed fruit	Salad	Ice cream	Vegetables	Seasonal
	Roti	Roti	with custard	Roti/Rice		Salad	Vegetables
	Rice	Rice				Rice	Bread
	Fruit salad						Caramel
							Custard

1. All curries, Biryanis, Pulaos, Pizzas, Cutlets etc., may include choices between vegetarian and non-vegetarian preparations. It is customary to serve non-vegetarian dishes at least twice a week.

2. Sweet is generally served at dinnertime when the diners are at ease, at the end of the day, in the above menu it is served every alternative day, but may be twice a week depending on the policy of the establishment.

3. Fruit is served at least once a day.

4. Salad as often as possible.

5. Accompaniments like papad, pickle, etc, are generally offered when no vegetable side dish is prepared, especially at lunch that is a hurried meal.

6. Anyone who wishes to have milk at teatime can order it specially.

7. Sunday breakfast is usually a heavier meal than on the other days, as people have more time to eat, and generally take breakfast later than usual.

Cyclic Menus have a Number of Advantages

(a) Once a basic menu pattern is established, the planner has more time for creative thinking in terms of adjustments that become necessary in case of holidays, special circumstances, staff shortage, delays in deliveries, and so on.

(b) The staff and work in kitchens and service areas get better organized because future production plans are known.

(c) Recipes get standardized with repeated preparation, making food service more cost effective for management and customers.

(d) Work can be equally distributed throughout the day so that tensions are reduced for kitchen staff irrespective of peaks and troughs in catering operations.

(e) Available equipment and skills can be optimally utilized if menus are thoughtfully planned in advance.

(f) Administrative work involved in ordering and stocking food is reduced, because a single order can be placed indicating timings for deliveries over a season.

Thus, a well-planned cyclic menu can be a very effective tool of management in a food service department. It should, however, have a degree of flexibility built into it, which can be made use of to introduce seasonal variations, special requirements (for the handicapped, aged, or sick), and to control waste.

Beverage Menu

The criteria used to prepare a wine menu or drinks list are the same as those used when preparing a food menu and as outlined earlier. The use of the wine menu or drinks list as a selling tool cannot be emphasized enough. Customers eating in a restaurant do not have to and will not embarrass if they do not purchase a drink. It is the caterer's ability to interest and gain the confidence of customers that is likely to lead them to purchase a drink. Beverage require fewer staff to process them and the profit from them higher than those from food and so it goes without saying that this is an area that requires time and attention from the caterer to obtain the full benefit.

Beverage lists should be specifically prepared for the particular unit in which they are being sold because the requirements vary greatly. The sales of wines and cocktails in hotels and restaurants are generally lower than they should be for such reasons as poor selling, overpricing and the snobbery that goes with wines and cocktails which tend to put customer ill at ease.

Types of Beverages Menu

The various types of beverages menus are numerous but for

simplicity they may be grouped as being of four kinds: wine menus, bar menus, room service beverage menus and special promotion beverage menus.

Wine Menus

Wine menus may be subdivided as follows:

Full Wine Menus

This kind of menus would be used in an up market hotel or restaurant where the customer's average spend would be high and where the time available to consume their meal would be likely to be in excess of one and a half hours. Like all menus a full wine menu is difficult to design. Certain wines must be on the menu if a restaurant is of a particular standing, it is the question of the selection of wines within the various types based on the manager's experience and the analysis of customer sales that make it difficult to keep a correct balance and restrict the choice to reasonable limits.

A full wine list may resemble a small book, often of fifteen to forty pages in length. Because of the size and cost it is often the practice to have the menu contained within a quality cover and to be of a loose-leaf form so that the individual pages may be updated when required and replaced. It is also the practice for many restaurants to give a brief description of the major types of wines as well as provide a map to show the origin of the wine. The price range for this type of menu is high because of the quality of the products.

Restricted Wine Menu

This kind of menu would be used in a middle type market operation where the demand for a full wine menu is very limited. It is also likely to be used when a highly skilled wine waiter is not required and where the waiting staff serves all food and beverages. The planning of a restricted wine menu is difficult and can best be done by an analysis of previous wine sales. It is usual that this type of menu would feature a few well known branded wines with which the majority of customer can identify. The price range for this type of menu would be lower than that of a full wine menu and would need to bear some relationship to the food menu prices.

Banquet/Function Menu

This type of menu is of the restricted type in that it will offer fewer wines than a full menu. The contents of the menu will depend on the type of banqueting being done but in general it is usual to offer a selection of wines with a varying price range so that it will suit a wide range of customers and their tastes. Again banqueting wine menus will usually list some well known branded wines. A point which must not be forgotten with branded wines is that customers frequently will know the prices charged for them in the local super market or wine store and therefore the caterer must be very careful as to the mark up on these wines so as not to create customer annoyance.

Bar Menus

These are basically of two types:

The large display of beverages and their prices, which is often located at the back of or to the side of bar and is often a legal requirement in many countries or small printed menu/list which is available on the bar and on the tables in the bar area. The large display of menus and prices would be in a general type of bar where the everyday types of drinks are served, the small printed menus being found in lounge and cocktail bars. The cocktail bar menu usually contains cocktails, mixed drinks, liqueurs and brandies, wine, and minerals and cordials. The layout for a cocktail bar menu need not follow any set order the emphasis for the layout being on merchandizing specific items.

Room Service Beverage Menu

The size and type of room service menu will depend on the standard of the hotel and the level of room service offered. For a luxury type unit the menu will be quite expensive, being a combination of items from the full wine list and from the bar list. In a middle type market unit the menu is likely to be quite small being a combination of items mainly from the bar list plus a few wines only from the restricted unit wine menu.

Because of the high labour costs for room service staff, a practice today in many hotels is to provide a small refrigerator in each bedroom stocked with limited quantity of basic drinks. There are many types of beverage units available specifically for use in bedrooms, some of which automatically records the removal of any item from the unit and records it as a charge to the customer.

Special Promotion Beverage Menu

This may take many forms from a free pre function reception to promote a particular beverage, to the promotion of pre lunch and pre dinner liqueurs by the use of attractive tent cards or to the promotion of the cocktails of the month. Frequently the suppliers willingly give assistance with beverage promotional menus by providing free advertising and promotional material and by offering the particular beverage free or at a special purchase price.

General Rules for Serving of Wines

The practice of serving a different kind of wine with each food course is seldom observed today other than for the very formal occasion or for a special gastronomic event. The choice of wine by a customer is highly individual and the once traditional rules of what wines should only be served with a particular food are not always observed today. Some aspects of the practice that have stood the test of time and are accepted and commonly practiced today are:

1. The progression of wines in a menu would be that light and delicate wines are served before fuller bodied wines, that simple wines are served before the higher quality wines and that young wines are served before the older wines.
2. When several wines are to be served with a menu the order of serving is normally accepted as being first a dry white wine followed by a red wine and finishing with sweet white wine.
3. Wines from several countries may be served with a meal providing that there is an affinity between the different wines and that they are accepted partners of food.
4. Champagne may be served throughout a meal with dry champagne being served with all courses other than with the sweet course when semi sweet champagne would be better suited.
5. Rose wines may also be served throughout a menu although it would be unusual for a formal or special gastronomic occasion.
6. Dry white wines are normally served with fish, shellfish and white meats such as poultry, pork.
7. Red wines are normally served with red meats.
8. Sweet white wines are normally served with cheese and desert.

Instruction of Menus

A menu needs to be constructed in a systematic manner. A list of the steps that can be followed is given below:

1. Decide on the menu pattern considered suitable in terms of its being set, selective, or a combination of both.

2. Decide on the degree of flexibility to be incorporated.
3. Write down the main dish and plan side dishes around it. The items selected should help to enhance the colour, texture, flavour and taste of the meal.
4. Menus should be checked vertically and horizontally in case of cyclic or weekly non-cyclic menus, to ensure that the same food item or dish does not appear consecutively on two or more days. It must not have the same item used twice in the same meal, nor on the same day. For example, avoid using mutton for lunch and dinner on the same day, or using potato for lunch as well as tea snacks.

The aim of every planner should be to create menus that will be fairly consistent in their quality characteristics, costs and therefore selling prices from day to day. To do this, seasonal and price fluctuations can be taken care of by selecting cheaper side dishes for expensive main dishes and vice versa, while at the same time complementing the main dish in flavour, taste, colour and texture. When choices are planned, the dishes chosen should be comparable in the 'value for money' that they provide, and in other aspects as necessary for particular customer requirements. Variations can be provided with the use of different cooking methods, seasonings or garnishing.

Selection of desserts should generally relate to the main course of the menu. If the latter is light, the dessert chosen can be rich, and vice versa. Desserts may be fruity, cooked puddings (hot or cold), creamy, such as ice-creams, soufflés, custards, kheers, or based on cakes, gelatin or pies, depending on the rest of the menu.

While there are meal times established for main meals, all food service establishments may not necessarily plan for full course meals. Small cafeterias, canteens, kiosks, mobile vans or vendors may cut down on menu items and provide plated meals, snacks and beverages. Such menus are becoming more and more popular as people want a bite between meals, when in company or while traveling. In addition, specialty menus that do not require changing are planned on popular demand. An appropriate example is the 'chaat' stall in India, where the same 'chaat' is prepared and served day after day because customers of all ages enjoy it. The popularity of such an establishment provides variety on the menu, through changes in ingredients and level of spicing rather than a change in the menu items. In fact, 'chaal' of any kind is such a hot favourite that a small comer set up in a cafeteria can become the source of customer attraction to the establishment.

The display of ingredients is also attractive and the dish is made on demand. This is a classic example of using favourite dishes on menus to increase acceptability and demand for other items, served in the cafeteria. Menu planning is thus an art involving knowledge, thought, insight, creativity and initiative, which with practice can become a very satisfying and profitable activity.

Menu Display

The menu can perform its rightful functions only if the customer can see and read it clearly on or before entering a food service establishment.

Menus may be displayed in many ways.

1. On a menu board with the help of plastic letters which can easily be re-arranged to change the name of the dish from day to day. Such a display is neat and clear. Its effect can be enhanced by using contrasts in colour such as white on black or red on white boards.
2. In small kiosks, canteens or mobile catering vans, menus are displayed on blackboards written out in chalk. The disadvantage is that customers brushing past can erase chalk.

3. Printed or neatly typed menus may be inserted in plastic cases and displayed. This method is often followed in coffee shops and cafeterias where a number of customers handle the menu to make their selections.

4. In hostels or other institutions typed menus are displayed on notice boards outside dining areas. This enables people to make up their mind about dishes before they go to service counters. The advantage lies in faster service and no unnecessary crowding, since those who do not like the menu do not enter the dining area. In such displays, it is preferable to have glass shutters so that the menu is visible and yet protected from dust and mishandling.

5. Printed booklets placed in attractive waterproof folders are a method of presenting menus to customers in restaurants offering extensive choices.

6. On formal occasions such as for banquets, small individual menu cards may be typed and placed on menu stands in front of each guest cover. Sometimes separate cards carrying the names of the guest are placed alongside. This enables invitees to be directed to their proper positions on the table without commotion, and also indicates to each diner what courses are being served. In this form of menu display, there are no price or portions printed along with the dishes, as the diners do not have to pay for their meals.

Five

Food and Beverage Production

Food production, whether for four persons or forty, is basically the same in terms of the quality desired by the consumer. Also the principles underlying the methods used for preparing and serving foods in large quantities remain unchanged. The difference lies in the larger volumes of food materials which have to be handled, combined, cooked, dished out and served imaginatively within a set cost structure and widely different tastes and requirements.

Food production encompasses the preparation of a large variety of items ranging from appetizers to curries, roasts, sandwiches, snacks, salads, vegetables and beverages. For each type of item, certain skills are needed and different methods of processing are required to produce different effects.

Food Production System

Food can be produced in quantity through a number of different ways, varying with the policy, size and type of catering establishment.

There are basically three types of food production systems:

(a) Conventional,

(b) Convenience, and

(c) Ready food system.

Conventional Food Systems

In this system food is produced totally from raw ingredients processed on the premises prior to service. Most small catering establishments and institutional kitchens follow this system in India. In the system all fresh food is ordered in a manner that it is delivered directly to the kitchens, or stored only for a day or two in refrigerated storage (depending on the volume). So relatively less storage space is required for food, than in other systems. The food is prepared from scratch, as it passes through the production cycle.

Convenience System

In this method of food production some of the food and ingredients used are bought pre-prepared or proportioned from the markets. Some of the items like soaps, noodles, marinated chicken, tandoori items require only finishing at the time of service, while others may be completely ready to serve not requiring processing at all. The latter include ice creams, sauces, salad dressings, fruit yogurts and sweets.

This system requires less preparation equipment, less space, energy and even fewer employees. But the ready foods purchased are costlier and require expensive cold and freezer storage facilities, with much more storage space than a conventional food system. The convenience system is used mostly by large hostels and multi-outlet food preparation centers.

Ready Food System

In this, the production of food is done continuously everyday, with no peaks and troughs. The system involves preparation of food into ready portions of individual food items or cooked dishes, which are then sealed and chilled, frozen and stored for use as and when required.

The ready food system works on the lines of a factory production system where foods are prepared, packed, freezer stored and transported to the points of use. It also involves additional expenses on cold and freezer storage and transportation. The issues of food also, have to be planned and coordinated very carefully because any food removed from freezer storage has to be used up and cannot be restored once thawed. In this system the food production shifts away from the service points. The greatest advantages f the system is that the quality and costs can be better controlled, and excessive handling of food at the point of use is prevented. This is possible because, only finishing kitchens are required at the points of service, which is therefore fast and safe.

Whatever system is adopted in an establishment, the basic process of food production remains the same, Food and ingredients have to be bought and then used for preparing the different dishes directly for service, or chilled and frozen for future use. The basic difference lies only in the location of the systems.

In fast food services the convenience and ready food systems are used to a large extent. Some large hotels may have their own ready food systems, but a large scale cook chill system is not likely to catch on in India, because of a number of reasons:

(i) There is a large variation in the methods of cooking and using food items and ingredients throughout the country, and many of the dishes do not lend themselves to standardization.

(ii) The feeding in hospitals and other institutions is not the total responsibility of professional caterers and managers, who can make decisions about the food service system.

(iii) Ready food systems require large investments and depend heavily on electricity for food preparation and storage, and its supply is very erratic all over the country.

(iv) A large percentage of the population (80%) in the country is still rural and people are looking for cheap foods with high satiety value, not expensive foods with standardization.

Therefore in considering which food system to use an establishment has to think of the price of the reduction that people will be wilting to pay.

Food Production Process

The process of food production involves a number of interdependent activities, including:

(a) Collecting the ingredients,
(b) Weighing and measuring them according to standard recipes,
(c) Preparing the different foods to make them ready for cooking,
(d) Cooking, and
(e) Dishing out for service.

Collecting Ingredients

In large quantity food preparation, collection of ingredients is done on the day previous to preparation. This is because some items have to be collected from the stores, while others are delivered directly to the kitchen such as milk and milk products, fresh fruits and vegetables. Timely collection also enables early preparation next morning. This helps to start off the next day without wasting time, in addition to distributing work evenly throughout the day. Further, in the event of a cook or assistant being absent the next day, the work goes on as per plan making it easier for others to handle the jobs without panicking.

Weighing and Measuring

In order to reproduce a popular dish each time a customer desires it, and to maintain standards of quality, it is important to weigh and measure ingredients accurately. In addition, the method of combining these ingredients using the desired methods of cooking at the right temperatures and for suitable periods of time, are essential for consistency. In other words, standard recipes are necessary for producing food in large quantities.

Preparation of Foods

All foods have to be prepared to some extent before they can be used immediately, stored, cooked, or served. The process of preparation generally involves activities like peeling, scraping, paring, cutting, grating, grinding, washing, sprouting, mixing serving and so on.

The following section deals with methods of preparing different foods prior to cooking, as well as forms in which they can be prepared to offer variety in textures.

Meats

The form in which meat may be prepared for cooking varies with the cut and the type of meat, such as top round, rib, leg and shoulder of pork, mutton, beef, etc. and the dish into which it is finally to be transformed for service, such as curries, kebabs, cutlets, roasts, tandoori, fritters, mince, pate, and so on. Meats may be cut into various sized pieces to suit the dish. For curries 100 g × 4 pieces is sufficient for a portion with or without bone. 1" cubes are used for kebabs, marinated overnight under refrigeration to be used the next day. Minced meat is steamed, spiced, bound, shaped into cutlets and used for frying and service immediately or stored for finishing on demand. Large joints may be coated with oil and stored under refrigeration for roasting the next day, rolled and boned meat may also be similarly treated. Chops may be trimmed, coated and prepared for frying, and so on.

119

Poultry

Pre-preparation consists of skinning and/or cutting dressed, drawn birds into portions. Chicken, generally, are cut into six portions (two legs or drumsticks, two thigh portions, two breast portions, but vary according to the dish for which they are being prepared. For tandoori or roast chicken, a full bird may be refrigerated, or four portions may be made (two leg-cum-thigh portions, plus two breast portions). These may then be marinated and kept ready in the refrigerator overnight to be roasted on demand. Whole birds when used for roasting can be portioned after cooking the process is generally known as 'carving'. Birds may be deboned for cutlets, fritters, or minced for making fingers or meatballs, etc.

Fish

Fish is generally frozen whole, filleted as such, or coated in breadcrumbs and kept ready for frying or grilling. Fish may be prepared into fish fingers or shredded for fritters and cutlets, or cut into small pieces for curried preparations. Other seafood may be similarly treated to prepare them for finishing when required.

Vegetables

Vegetables may be prepared in a number of forms depending on the end use to which they are put and their contribution to the whole meal. For instance, when vegetables form the main dish of a menu, they may be prepared whole, plain, or stuffed, as required. As side dishes, they may be chopped into various shapes and sizes, depending on the texture and consistency of the main dish that they are accompanying. The preparation of vegetables may be conveniently dealt with fewer than three headings, namely leafy vegetables, root vegetables and other vegetables.

Leafy Vegetables

These are generally prepared on the same day as the meal service, since they contain a high proportion of moisture, and easily shrivel up when prepared. Quite a few green vegetables are used as herbs and garnishes, and in the preparation of sauces and chutneys. Some are used as side dishes in a menu, or even as an ingredient in the preparation of main dishes. For example, spinach may be ground and added to dough for making spinach roti, or added to pulses, etc. Vegetables may also be prepared as main dishes, or served along with meat. In large food service establishments, leafy vegetables, especially the dark green ones, may be lightly steamed, cooled, packed, and frozen for use when required. This is a very handy way of preserving their colour and flavour, instead of allowing them to shrivel up or brown due to enzymatic activity. It is not always possible in large-scale food production to receive deliveries of leafy vegetables on the same day as they are required and therefore, all preparation methods must aim it maintaining their quality at the optimum level. Some green vegetables acts only as flavouring agents, and are therefore used as garnishes, such as mint, parsely, green coriander, etc. They may, however, be used as ingredients in food preparations such as in mint raita, chutney, pulao, roti, etc. Green garnishes ire best washed, placed on a clean cloth, and the cloth twisted to wring out all adhering moisture. The eaves are then finely chopped, packed in polythene bags, frozen, and then used as garnishes over dished out food, or for incorporation in any dish.

Root Vegetables

As the name indicates, vegetables that mature under the soil fall in this category of vegetables and are hardier than other vegetables. Some commonly used root vegetables are potatoes, onions, carrots, garlic, beetroot, etc. Since these vegetables are hardy they can withstand chopping, peeling, grating, slicing and shaping much better than other vegetables. They also take to mechanical handling more easily and can therefore be prepared for cooking with the help of kitchen machines.

Other Vegetables

This group includes all other vegetables that do not come under the first two categories. Some examples are stem vegetables like lotus, banana and rhubarb stalks; gourds such as green, ridge and snake gourds; pumpkin, courgettes, brinjals, beans, cucumber, drumsticks, mango green, tomato and flowers of plants like water lilly, banana flowers lady's finger, salad vegetables, etc.

The list can be exhaustive as different plants and their parts are grown and used as food in different parts of the world.

The most succulent vegetables can be prepared by just peeling and cutting them into attractive sized pieces, scooping them out and then cooking and serving them as stuffed vegetables.

Cooking

Once the food items have been prepared, they need to be put together or combined to form a dish that is attractive, aromatic, tasty, and thus enjoyable to eat. Most foods need to be subjected to some process involving the application of heat, in order to make them tender, easy to digest, and safe from microorganisms. The process of subjecting foods to the action of heat is termed as 'cooking'. Some foods need not be cooked if the desired effect required is crispness, as in salad making, or if they are to be used as accompaniments or garnishes for main dishes.

The manner in which heat is applied to food during cooking determines the type of cooking method used. The methods developed may be classified under three main heads as shown.

Moist Heat	Dry Heat	Combination Method
Boiling	Roasting	Braising
Simmering	Grilled, Broiling	
Poaching	Toasting	
Stewing	Baking	
Blanching	Sautéing	
Steaming	Frying	
Pressure Cooking	Microwave Cooking	

Moist Heat Methods

Boiling

Boiling is cooking foods by just immersing them in water at 100°C and maintaining the water at that temperature till the food is tender. Water is said to be boiling when large bubbles are seen rising constantly to the surface of the liquid and then breaking rapidly. Foods may be boiled in any liquid that is bubbling at the surface such a stock, milk, juices, syrups, etc. Boiling is rarely used as the sole method of cooking, except to prepare foods for further treatment in meal preparation. The few food that are cooked by boiling and served as such are potatoes, eggs, sweet potatoes, rice and beetroot. Meats may sometimes be served after cooking in boiling liquid such as in the preparation of stews.

Boiling of food may be done in one of two ways:

(i) By bringing the water or liquid bubbling point and then adding the food to be cooked, and allowing the liquid to bubble again till the food is done,

(ii) By adding the food to water or liquid and heating them together to the boiling point of the liquid and then maintaining that temperature till the food is tender.

Boiling as a method of cooking is generally used in combination with simmering and other methods in the preparation of curries, soups, stews, casseroles and foods cooked in sauces.

Simmering

When foods are cooked at temperatures just below the boiling point of the liquid in which they are immersed, the process is known as "simmering". It is a useful method to use when food has to be cooked for a long time to make it tender, as in the case of cheaper cuts of meat used for stews or stock preparation.

Poaching

This involves cooking in the minimum amount of liquid at a temperature just below the boiling point. Foods generally poached are eggs, fruits and fish. For poaching eggs, the addition of a little salt and vinegar to the cooking liquid lowers the temperature of coagulation, cooking eggs quickly and giving the poached egg a clean smooth edge.

Stewing

This is a gentle method of cooking in a pan with a tight fitting lid, using small quantities of liquid, to cover only half the food. The steam generated within the pan thus cooks the food above the liquid. The liquid is brought to the boiling point and then the heat applied is reduced to maintain the cooking at simmering temperature, that is 98°C. Stewing is therefore a slow method taking from 2 to 4 hours depending on the nature and volume of foods being stewed. The method is generally used for cooking cheaper cuts of meat (less tender cuts) along with some root vegetables and legumes, all put in the same cooking pot and cooked in stock or water. The longer cooking time and the lower temperatures enable tougher meat fibers to become tender. The cooking of meat and vegetables together make the dish attractive and nutritious since no liquid is discarded.

Blanching

In meal preparation it is often necessary only to peel off the skin of fruits, vegetables, nuts, etc. without making the food tender. This is achieved by dipping the food in boiling water for varying periods of time (5 seconds to 2 minutes) depending on the texture of the food to remove the skin or peel without softening the food. Pouring enough boiling water on the food to immerse it for some time, or subjecting foods to boiling temperatures for short periods and then immediately immersing in cold water kept ready for the purpose also does blanching. The process causes the skin to become loose and can be peeled off easily. The process helps to maintain a good texture, while improving the colour and flavour of foods. In addition the peels can be easily removed to improve digestibility, eliminate enzyme and microbial activity, and make it safe for consumption in salads, sandwiches, puddings or even to be eaten a dessert fruit.

Steaming

As the term indicates, this method requires the food to be cooked in steam generated from vigorously boiling water or liquid in a pan so that the food is completely surrounded by steam, and not in contact with the water or liquid. Steaming is generally done in special equipment designed for the purpose. Small establishments can use double boilers, while larger ones utilize pressure cookers designed to hold 16-20 liters of liquid, and provided with separators for steaming food. For very large establishments, steamers are available which may be simple or pressure steamers for quick cooking of large quantities of food. This method of cooking is best suited for dishes that need to be served soon after steaming, that are, piping hot. Foods best suited are vegetables, fruits, fish, custards, cereals, and generally those that get tender quickly. The method is ideal for making idlis, dhokla or other fermented products. Steaming equipment is now available which can turn out 100 to 120 portions of steamed food in 10 to 15 minutes.

Steaming has certain definite advantages of making foods more easily digestible, nutritious and full of flavour. This is because it is not necessary to add fat in this process, and the food retains its nutrients better because heating temperatures are constant, cooking time short and leaching minimum. Besides, it is consumed as soon as it is prepared, especially if the food is batch cooked according to demand. This prevents nutrient losses, which would normally take place if the food is held for some time before being served.

Pressure Cooking

This is a method of cooking developed on the principle that more heat is generated by steam under pressure than otherwise, and therefore cooking time is greatly reduced. Also, since the steam is not allowed to escape, the volatile flavour compounds remain in the food and the shorter cooking time enhances nutrient retention and palatability. Pressure-cooking is best suited to cooking of foods that are required to be moist such a curries, soups, broth and stews. The equipment for pressure-cooking varies in its capacity to suit the needs of food services of different types and sizes, and can usually be adjusted for pressures of 5-10-15 Ibs per square inch.

Dry Heat Methods

Roasting

This is a method in which the food is brought in contact with direct heat from a flame or any source of radiant heat. The food is periodically coated with fat and the pieces of food, generally meats, are turned over the fire occasionally for even cooking. Roasting may be carried out using three types of equipment. When a 'spit' containing live coals on which meat pieces, skewed together are placed and rotated at intervals using the wooden or heat proof handles on the skewer, the method of cooking is known as 'spit roasting'. 'Boti' kebabs are prepared in this manner. For spit roasting, it is advisable to use small pieces of deboned meats to ensure proper and even cooking. The meat cooked in this manner is called 'barbecued' meat, and has an even brown colour with a characteristic flavour. It also has high customer appeal because it is served straight from the fire and is fresh, hot and aromatic. The second type of roasting is done in an oven, either electric, or a mud oven known as the 'tandoor' and the method is referred to as 'oven roasting'. This is a common method because of the ease with which a large amount of meat or poultry can be roasted. In this the meat is usually placed on a meshed or slatted shelf inserted in a roasting tray, to allow the meat drippings to fall to the base of the tin during cooking. If the drippings are allowed to touch the base of the meat, charring or burning will take place, or part of the meat will get the flavour of fried meat. The drippings are, however, used to moisten meat from time to time.

In 'oven roasting', usually large joints or full birds are cooked. The meat turns brown and crisp on the surface and moist and tender inside. If the top is also required to be moist then birds are best roasted with their skins. Good roasting involves preheating the oven to 425°C first, placing the meat in it, and letting it brown for 5-10 minutes and then reducing the temperature and allowing it to cook till tender. If only one temperature is used, then cooking at a moderate temperature of 350°C to 375°C for a longer period gives a better product than a high temperature for a shorter time. This is because moderate temperatures and longer cooking time ensures complete heat penetration through the food. Constant high temperatures may even lead to over browning or charring and uneven cooking, with greater moisture loss resulting in a dry product. It is a good practice to oven-roast joints after browning them first, and then wrapping them in aluminum foil. This method retains moisture and flavours better and leads to even heat penetration and cooking.

Roasting can also be done in a heavy pan if small joints are to be cooked. Enough fat is healed in the pan to cover its base. The meat is then browned in the hot fat by turning it occasionally to cook it evenly on all sides. It is then lifted out and placed on top of skewers, positioned at the base of the pan to prevent the joints from sticking to the base of the utensil. The meat should only just touch the fat. The pan is then covered with a tight fitting lid, and the meal allowed cooking on a slow fire till tenders. Often root vegetables may be prepared and added to the pan before putting the lid and allowed lo roast along with the meat. This method is known as 'pan or pot roasting'. The principle underlying the process of roasting involves sealing the meat surface through the coagulation of surface proteins brought about by direct radiant heat and high temperature. The sealing prevents further evaporation of moisture from the inside of the meat, retaining its juices and natural flavour. Besides meat, root vegetables like potatoes and sweet potatoes may be oven or pan roasted. In India, peanuts, popcorn and Bengal gram are often roasted in a 'kadai' containing sand or salt those are continuously heated over a source of heat. After roasting is complete, the sand or salt are separated by sieving and the nuts and roasted gram vended.

Grilling and Broiling

The terms 'grilling' and 'broiling' are used synonymously for cooking by application of dry heat. The food is placed on a metal grid directly over the source of heat or on a tray placed under the source of heat. Some equipment is designed so that food comes between electrically heated grill bars or hot plates. Usually tender cuts of meal, poultry or fish are prepared this way, and browned under a grill. Cheese and meat preparations like pizza, cheese toasts, chops, bacon, sausages, tomatoes, capsicums, etc. are also grilled. In fact, this method of cooking has given the name to the dish known as 'Mixed Grill', which consists of a variety of meats and vegetables grilled and served on a platter with salad and cereal. When food is cooked uncovered on heated metal or a frying pan, the methods often known as 'pan-broiling'.

Grilling has also been done with the use of infrared radiations reducing the cooking time. The equipment used for this purpose is called the 'infra-red grill'.

Toasting

The term 'toasting' is used to describe a process by which bread slices are kept under a grill, or between two heated elements, to brown on both sides and become crisp. This does not imply cooking. Masters are now available which radiate heat from both sides on the bread at the same time, and can be adjusted to give the required degree of brownness through temperature controls. Automatic models switch off when the preset temperature and brownness is reached, and the toasts pop out of the toaster automatically.

Baking

Foods cooked by baking involve the use of oven or tandoor equipment in which hot air circulates around the food placed in it. While it is basically a dry heat method of cooking, the action of dry heat is combined with that of steam that is generated while the food is cooking. Foods baked are generally brown and crisp on the top, and soft and porous in the centers. Some dishes baked are cakes, breads, puddings, vegetables, meat dishes in sauce, etc.

The principle involved in baking is, that the air inside the oven is heated by a source of heat, either electricity, gas, or wood, as in the case of the tandoor. The oven is insulated to prevent outside temperatures from causing fluctuations in internal temperature of the equipment. In the case of the traditional 'tandoor' lie insulation is provided by a coating of mud given on the outside and inside of the galvanized iron or brick oven. The temperature of the traditional oven is tested by experience; the indicator being the speed with which water sprinkled on the inside evaporates. If it is too high further sprinkling is done to reduce the temperature just right for the cooking of specific foods. Once the right temperature is attained, the foods are placed in the hot air currents which pass on their heat to the food through the container, or directly as the case may be. The top of the food gets brown and crisp because f the direct heat on the surface of the food.

The methods of heat transfer involved are radiation from the source of heat to the metal wall at the base if the oven; by conduction from the base to other walls; and by convection through the heated air currents et up in the oven, to the food.

Sautéing

This method involves cooking in just enough fat or oil to cover the base of the pan. The food is tossed occasionally or turned over with a spatula to enable all the pieces to come in contact with the oil and get cooked evenly. Sautéing involves lightly tossing the food in heated oil and then covering the an with a lid, reducing the flame or intensity of the heat applied to the pan, and allowing the food to be cooked till tender in its own steam. The product obtained in cooking by this method is slightly moist, tender nit without any liquid or gravy. Foods cooked by sautéing are generally vegetables, used as side dishes i a menu. Sautéing can, however, be well combined with other methods of cooking to produce variety in meals.

Frying

This is a method in which the food to be cooked is immersed fully or partially in hot fat, till it acquires a golden brown colour and a crisp feel. When foods are completely immersed in the fat or oil, the method is known as 'deep frying', while the term 'shallow frying' is used when the food is only partially immersed or has only surface contact with the oil or fat.

Foods are generally fried in a 'kadai' or in fryers designed for the purpose, and provided with wire nets for immersing the food in the hot fat and then draining out the excess oil from the food after the cooking is completed.

Fried foods have always been favourites with all age groups. Some fried foods are fish and chips, fried chops, kebabs, cutlets, fritters, samosas, and so on. The list can be endless because fried foods are crisp, attractive, aromatic, quickly served and microbial safe due to the high temperature at which the cooking is done. In addition to the above characteristics, good quality deep fried foods provide a lot of variety in menus. For example, potatoes can be served as fingers, crisps, chips, fritters, pakodas cutlets and bondas. Without these choices available to the caterer and customer meal production as well as consumption would become a monotonous task. Fried foods also prove to be cheaper to produce in large quantities, in terms of time, labour and money, because they are quick cooking and can be produced at short notice if preparation is well planned, and the partly prepared portions are stored at the right temperatures for safety. The ordering of ingredients for fried foods becomes more specific in relation to size, type and variety of a food portion required, thus leading to better cost and quality control. For example, when purchasing fish fillets a specific order can be placed such a 100×250 g fillets of the specific fish required. In contrast, if a total order of 25 kg fish is placed, it can include pieces of varying sizes leading to inefficient portion control and wastage during frying.

Deep fried foods differ greatly in texture, flavour, appearance and taste. Since each food has special quality characteristics it is important to maintain or enhance them in the process of frying. To do this it is essential to know what deep-frying involves and how quality can be affected for better or for worse.

The factors involved are:

(i) *Selection of the right frying medium*: Any fat or oil used for frying should be flavourless so that it does not mask the natural flavour of the food. The smoking point of the frying medium when fresh should not be less than 220°C, and it must contain some antioxidant and stabilizer to prevent its deterioration during storage, and while in use.

(ii) *Knowledge of the right frying temperatures*: Different foods require different frying temperatures for best results. If higher temperatures are used than necessary, the oil or fat breaks down and discolours the food, making it unacceptable and unpalatable.

(iii)   *Use of proper frying techniques*: The proper methods used in frying are vital to the quality of t product obtained. If foods have been fried properly there will be minimum absorption of fat or oil by I food, making it look and taste crisp and fresh instead of stale and greasy. Foods that look greasy indicate that they have been fried at too low a temperature or refried to serve hot. Most foods require t be coated before frying in order to retain moisture and flavour, and seal in the nutrients. Some coating materials that can be used are:

(a)   A mixture of flour and milk;

(b)   A batter of flour, milk and eggs;

(c)   Finely rolled dough as in the case of turnovers and samosas

(d)   Egg and vermicelli; and

(e)   Gram flour batter.

Sweets can also be cooked by the method of frying, such as doughnuts, gulab-jamuns, shahi tukre, pineapple fritters, etc. Any method used for frying requires knowledge of the composition of various oils and fats and how best they can be conserved before, while and after cooking; and how best various foods can be coated to get the most acceptable products. In addition, skill is necessary to prepare the coatings of the right consistencies and composition to suit the natural qualities of the food being fried and to try and enhance them, e.g. the moisture content of foods, their tenderness, and degree of shrinkage or expansion occurring during the process.

(iv)   *Proper care and selection of frying equipment*: Selection of the right size and design for the equipment to suit the needs of an establishment is important especially when a fryer has to be invested on. The size will be determined by the frequency with which fried foods appear on the menu and the volume of frying to be done in one lot.

The principles underlying cooking of foods by frying are:

(a) Very rapid heat transfer takes place from the frying medium to the food.

(b) Part of the fat combines with the cooked food to provide flavour and nutrients.

(c) The high temperature browns the surface of the food; the moisture is lost faster from the surface to provide a firm seal. This keeps the inside of the fried food moist and tender and helps to retain the natural flavour of the food.

The skills required in the actual process of frying can be learnt easily with practice if one is made aware of the hazards that can occur from careless handling of fats and oils and hot equipment.

The basic skills involve a thorough knowledge of the principles outlined above, and those listed below:

(a) Knowledge of various oils suitable for frying and their smoking points.

(b) Correct temperatures for frying of different foods.

(c) Level of frying medium in the equipment, to prevent splashing of hot oil or fat while frying.

(d) Heating medium gradually and then increasing temperature to that required for frying.

(e) Shape and size of foods fried should be same as far as possible, to obtain uniform browning.

(f) Knowledge of correct quantities to be fried at one time in relation to size of equipment. This also ensures even heat penetration. About one and a half to twice the fat weight can generally be fried in one hour. In a good fryer, the food fat ratio can be 1:5 to 1:8, depending on the food.

(g) Salting destroys crispness and therefore should preferably be done prior to service.

(h) Maintenance of frying equipment is important for increasing its efficiency and producing evenly fried and dry products.

(i) Turning foods while frying them requires skill to prevent splashing of hot oil.

(j) Knowledge of the qualities of food that make them suitable for frying.

(k) Proper draining of oil from products after frying.

(l) Awareness of the hazards, and equipment necessary to prevent accidents.

(v) *Microwave Cooking*: This method of cooking involves the use of high frequency electromagnetic waves (microwaves), which penetrate the food and produce frictional heat by setting up vibrations within the food. Special ovens are designed for the purpose. These are fitted with a magnetron so placed as to focus the microwaves on to the food. The two greatest advantages of cooking by this method are quick cooking (within minutes), and the absence of heat in the oven. The latter enables dishes to be removed from the oven with ease and safely without the use of oven clothes or gloves. The method is however only suitable for cooking or heating up small portions. It is an excellent method for reheating or finishing individual portions of food on demand, because the method does not brown the food each time it is heated, and hence retains the original colour of the food. In some models of the microwave oven a browning or roasting cycle has been introduced where required in finishing kitchens.

In microwave cooking however, it is important to remember that metals reflect the microwaves, while glass, plastic, paper or china transmits them, to the food. It is therefore necessary to use cooking containers that will transmit the microwaves.

The usefulness of microwave oven in self-service cafeterias, kiosks, coffee shops and lunchrooms, where people eat at different limes and in small groups, cannot be overemphasized. In industrial and hospital canteens where services need to be provided for night staff, the microwave is an asset for healing up meals at odd hours, in required qualities and instantly.

Combination Methods

These methods involve the use of more than one method of cooking. The most commonly used combination method of cooking is 'Braising'.

Braising

This is a method in which roasting and stewing are combined for cooking. The foods are first browned or pan roasted in little oil or fat to seal off the surface, then half covered with liquid, the pan tightly closed, and the food stewed till tender. Braising is a good method, especially for cooking meats, and a lot of Indian curries are prepared this way. Similarly, legumes and pulses may be sautéed in a little at, and then pressure-cooked or steamed. Another commonly used example of a combination method of cooking is the preparation of meatball curry. In this, mincemeat is mixed with herbs, spices, onions, garlic and Bengal gram dal, and pressure-cooked till tender. The mixture is then ground to a fine paste, bound agether with egg, made into balls and deep-fried curry, is then prepared by browning onions adding spices, tomato puree and water. The mixture is then brought to a boil, and them eat balls added to it. The aperture is then held just below boiling for a few minutes, and the mixture simmered and held hot for service. It is thus seen that two or more methods may be used together in preparing a dish. The methods of cooking discussed above require the application of heat to foods, but methods of food preparation involving the removal of heat from foods are also used in food preparation, such as in the case of chilled and frozen dishes like cold soups, desserts, jellies, souffles, moulded salads and ice-creams to mention just a few.

Effect of Preparation and Cooking Methods

Moist methods lead to relatively greater losses of nutrients than dry methods of cooking, but some nutrients are stable than others as far as heat, temperatures and lime of cooking are concerned. Proteins, fats and carbohydrates are not lost in day to day cooking of foods, but in vegetables that contain higher moisture content, water-soluble vitamins are vulnerable to destruction by heat or loss through leaching n the cooking water. This is more so if salt is added to the cooking water and then discarded, because along with water-soluble vitamins, the mineral salts of sodium, potassium, and chlorine are also leached out of the food. It is therefore advisable to cook in a minimum amount of water, or to utilize any excess water in soups and gravies. Root vegetables do not lose nutrients through leaching to the extent that other vegetables do because hey are generally boiled in their skins. Losses due to oxidation and evaporation occur more when vegetables are peeled and cut a long time before cooking. The size of the pieces also determines the degree of loss. The greater the surface area of the food exposed, the greater will be the losses.

The cooking time and amount of liquid are important factors in nutrient retention too, and methods of cooking should aim it the shortest possible time and minimum amount of water used in the process. The best nutrient retention n cooking vegetables is achieved when they are sautéed in a little fat or oil and allowed to steam in their own moisture on a low fire till tender. Spices may be added before the steaming process. Steaming under pressure is the fastest way of cooking food, and an important equipment to have in kitchens is the steamer and pressure cooker.

All foods need to be washed before they are cooked, and some even require soaking for different time periods. Water-soluble components do get lost to various extents even during these treatments. It is therefore advisable to wash foods as little as is necessary for cleaning them and utilize the soaking water in the cooking process.

The most easily destroyed vitamins during cooking is vitamin C, because it gets easily oxidized, in addition to dissolving in washing and cooking water. The best way to conserve this vitamin is therefore to cook covered for very short periods. The best of course, is to offer the food containing this vitamin uncooked forms such as ripe fruits, and salad vegetables. The only food whose nutritional qualities not get affected during cooking is egg.

Vitamin A or carotene is relatively stable to heat and therefore cooking by moist methods does not affect these nutrients. Dry heat methods are, however, destructive, especially shallow frying or roasting. The losses are not due so much to the heat applied, as they are to air exposure for long periods. In deep-frying, where the exposure to air is less, oxidative losses are reduced.

Any discussion of the effects of cooking on the nutritional qualities of foods would be incomplete without briefly mentioning the methods that can enhance the nutrient quality of foods if followed in for preparation activity. These are briefly outlined in table and provide a useful guide to enhancing nutritional quality without increasing costs.

Enhancing the nutritive value of foods alone is not enough; it is important to ensure that food preparation methods make the nutrients available for ready absorption through improved digestibility of the foods prepared. For example, a food may contain all the desired nutrients, but if it is fried in oil that has been repeatedly used for frying, the food prepared in it may become toxic and difficult to digest, although when it is served hot it may be acceptable to the customer.

Table 5.1: Enhancing Nutritive Value of Foods

Methods	Foods Involved	Effect
Germination or Sprouting	Pulses, grains, legumes, edible seeds of proteins. Increase in B-Vitamins	Development of Vitamin C improved biological value
Fermentation	Doughs, cereal-pulse mixtures, beverages.	Enhancement of B-vitamins Digestibility improves
Supplementation	Combination of foods which supplement each other in nutritive value like dishes of cereals and pulses cooked in combination; or cereals and vegetables; cereals and milk	Total value of the dish or meal is increased nutrients added by each of the food combined.
Fortification	Processed food products with iodine and potassium, oils with vitamin D and so on at the processing stage	Increase in the nutrient which is added to the food
Enrichment	Processed food products the food processed is brought up to the value of the raw food.	The nutritive value of

Knowledge of the beneficial effects of cooking and the characteristics of certain food components is important to successful food production.

The benefits are:

(i) Cooking improves the appearance of many foods and helps to develop flavours in them.

(ii) Cooking destroys pathogenic organisms that may be present, making the food safe for consumption,

(iii) The digestibility of starchy foods is enhanced through the release of starch and other nutrients from the grains of cereals, making the food more easily accessible to digestive enzymes. Cooking also inhibits undesirable changes from taking place in foods by inactivating those enzymes that produce them.

(iv) Cooking makes foods like meat tender and much easier to chew, digest and absorb,

(v) Some foods contain substances known as anti-vitamins that interfere with the utilization of nutrients by the body. For example, egg white contains a substance called avidin that inactivates the vitamin biotin of egg yolk, if raw egg is eaten. Cooking destroys avidin making the vitamin available to the body. Also some pulses contain enzyme inhibitors, which if not destroyed by cooking make the food indigestible. Therefore, while sprouting or germination enhances the vitamin values of pulses, the sprouts should always be steamed lightly before adding to salads, because the raw pulse protein will not be digested due to the presence of the trypsin inhibitor. (Trypsin is the digestive enzyme, which acts on the protein of foods).

In general, moderate heating used in cooking improves the biological value of proteins in foods. Excessive heating, however, can denature the proteins, making them unavailable.

Cooking Techniques

Whatever method of cooking is chosen for the preparation of foods, certain techniques can be developed through knowledge and experience to help in utilizing available resources more efficiently.

Techniques for Preparation

(i) Cutting vegetables on a chopping board with a sharp heavy knife makes chopping of large quantities easier, rhythmic, even safe, and quicker as against cutting each piece of vegetable by holding it in the hand and manipulating the knife. Similarly, peeling is smoother and faster with a peeler than with a knife. Using egg and tomato slices gives even slices, and they are quick to use. Gadgets are available which can be used to shape freshly boiled eggs (while they are still hot) into a square shape, for even square slices to add variety in garnishing.

(ii) While preparing dough in quantity, a kneading machine, or dough hook attachment fixed to a kitchen machine is handy, safe and quick.

(iii) While dividing dough for a hundred portions, it may be rolled out into a cylindrical shape with the palm of the hand, and then rhythmically cut into one-inch portions. This would ensure even sizes of whatever has to be made from the dough.

(iv) To make cutlets in large quantity, they can be shaped, coated and breaded and kept ready for frying on demand.

(v) Some foods which require a long time and effort to peel, and for which there is no machine available as yet, need to be handled with initiative. A typical example is the peeling of ginger and garlic, which is used in such small quantities in cooking that even if there were a machine for the job, it would not be worth investing on. The cumbersome task of flaking garlic and peeling ginger, which comes in such irregular shapes, can be handled by peeling both these spices when staff are relatively free, and preserving them in large quantities in white vinegar to be used when required. Wrapping garlic pods in a clean kitchen cloth and rolling over with a rolling pin loosens the outer fine covering and makes garlic easier and quicker to peel by rubbing the pods between the thumb and index finger. Ginger may be cut into fine strips or large chunks and preserved in vinegar for use. In short, selecting the right equipment for a particular use and developing ways of using both equipment and foods effectively are the basis of efficiency when dealing with large quantity food production.

Techniques for Cooking

(i) Planning menus to contain dishes that require different temperatures so that they can be placed on different shelves of the same oven is a time and saving technique for meal preparation. This is because, usually, the topmost shelf has the highest temperature (especially in non-convection ovens), while the lowermost shelf has the lowest temperature. This technique also helps to utilize the equipment optimally.

(ii) Placing dishes that require different methods of cooking in one meal so that when one dish is being cooked in the oven, another is done on the cooking range on the top of the oven. While that is being done, the accompaniments can be prepared and so on.

(iii) Using power equipment where possible to keep fatigue and anxiety to a minimum, such as steamers, kitchen machines, ovens, etc.

(iv) Using modular equipment that can fit into the refrigerator for storage, into the oven for cooking and the bainmarie for holding prior to service. This not only saves time but also decreases the volume of dishwashing, reducing both effort and the expense on detergents.

(v) Using the heat of switched off ovens or hotplates to dry off meringues, or bread for crumbs. This list of techniques can be extended according to the activities and needs of individual establishments, but a few examples of analyzed activities focusing on usually time-consuming tasks show the advantages of using certain techniques, in terms of utilizing materials, time and effort for greater efficiency.

Effective Use of Leftovers

When food remains unsold in large quantities it usually gets pilfered, or wasted through mishandling and spoilage, unless it is reused in some way and presented to the customer again. Since already cooked food cannot be stored for too long, without its quality deteriorating, it is important to devise ways of incorporating it as soon as possible into new dishes, dishes in which the food is completely unrecognizable. Yet, there must be no relaxation in terms of the standards of quality offered to the customer.

Leftover

Tandoori Chicken

This can be used as such or deboned and the meat used as an ingredient in the next meal or on the next day's menu.

Some ideas for its use are discussed below.

In boned form the possibilities are:

(a) In chicken salad.
(b) Converted into curried or butter chicken.
(c) Chicken biryani or fried rice.

In deboned form the chicken may be utilized in the following ways:

(a) Minced and mixed with binding ingredients, shaped into chicken balls or fingers and deep fried to be served as a snack.
(b) As balls they may also be used curried, with noodles or other pasta dishes and served as a main or side dish.
(c) The chicken can be minced and converted into a sandwich spread.
(d) As such, deboned chicken can be mixed with steamed or sautéed vegetables to make a good side dish.

(e) For making chicken stew.

(f) Chicken soup with sweet corn.

(g) Sweet and sour chicken.

(h) In the preparation of pizzas, pulaos, stuffed paranthas, samosas, turnovers.

Leftover Vegetable Pulao

This can be converted into:

(a) Vegetable balls or bondas, cutlets or tikkis to be used as snack.

(b) Curried balls generally termed as 'koftas' in Indian cooking.

(c) Minced and used as coating or covering for cheese pakoras or fritters, scotch eggs, nargisi koftas, etc.

(d) Mixed with white sauce, and covered with cooking cheese and baked in the oven.

Leftover Curds

These may be used for preparing the following:

(a) Marinade for meats, fish, poultry and cottage cheese.

(b) Gravies for curry preparations.

(c) Sandwich spread or dips for snacks, by passing through a fine muslin and allowing the sour water to drain off. This water may be separately used for adding to fresh milk for cheese (cottage)

(d) Dough which need to be fermented for making naan, fried poories called 'bhaturas' and other types of fermented breads.

(e) Fresh curds by using a bit of the left over one as a starter.

(f) Sour beverages like 'lassi' common in tropical climates during the hot season.

(g) Curd rice.

(h) Raitas.

Leftover Tomato Onion Salad

The tomato and onion slices may be separated and incorporated into dishes as an ingredient or used as garnishes. Some suggestions for their use are:

(a) Soups
(b) Curries
(c) Sauces
(d) Dry mixed vegetables
(e) Pizzas
(f) Stuffed omelettes
(g) Garnishes

The above examples indicate the unending possibilities of using up leftovers while still maintaining high standards of quality in terms of freshness, appearance, colour, texture and therefore acceptability. All that is required is creativity, vigilance regarding proper methods of storage and a policy to us leftovers tot later than the following day.

In large food service establishments, extra portions can be diverted for immediate service to inmates of social institutions like homes for the handicapped, orphanages, etc. so that there will be no leftovers it the end of any day. Such policies help to provide quality food at a standard of skill that such institutions would not normally be able to afford. At the same time the food cost can be recovered from the institutions of which the food is diverted and wastage is prevented.

Holding Techniques

Every food service establishment requires holding prepared food for varying periods of time before it is served. This is necessitated by the fact that all foods cannot be prepared quickly enough to serve on demand, and customers do not all come at the same time. The basic principles underlying the holding of foods are:

1. To maintain them at temperatures that prevent microbial activity and ensure their safety for consumption. Foods must, therefore, either be held above 63°C or below 5°C. As a general rule it would be safe to serve hot foods boiling hot and cold foods really chilled or frozen.

2. Holding techniques must maintain the quality characteristics of food such as quantitative, sensory and nutritional.

Very often, foods prepared too early and thus held too long, tend to lose their moisture and shrink because of the constant heat applied to them. This affects the appearance, colour, flavour and the size of le portion that can be served, deviating from the standards expected by the customer. Hence the importance of preparing foods, keeping them in readiness for cooking as close to serving time as possible. Batch cooking therefore has specific advantages.

Methods of Holding Foods

1. Salads, desserts, sauces, milk and milk-based dishes must be held in refrigerated equipment.

2. Soups, curries, hot desserts and custards should be held in preheated bainmaries designed to maintain food at safe temperatures.

3. Ice-creams must be held at 3°C in refrigerated case maintained at that temperature. Sometimes, bulk ice-cream containers may be kept in salt-ice mixtures to maintain their temperatures, quality and safety. Frozen desserts, especially milk based ones, once melted must never be refrozen as they can prove a serious health hazard.

Food production, thus, involves stringent measures and close supervision at every step to ensure that the food obtained, prepared, held and served is wholesome and safe for consumption.

Beverage Production Methods

The term beverage in this context is used to describe both alcoholic and non-alcoholic drinks. The degree of preparation necessary before these different beverages can be served to the customer varies but in the majority of cases it is the non-alcoholic beverages that fall into the categories of raw and semi prepared products and the alcoholic beverages that are in the main already fully prepared.

1. *Raw beverages*. These are beverage products that required a higher degree of preparation, in comparison to the other categories, before beings served to the customer. Examples of such beverages are tea, coffee, cocoa, which may required up to fifteen minutes before reaching a ready-to-serve state.

   The preparation of these raw beverage products may be away from the service area and customer, for example a stillroom in the kitchen of a large hotel, although in some specialty restaurants or coffee shops the tea or coffee making facilities may be an integral part of the total food service being offered by the catering operation.

2. *Semi-prepared*: These are beverage products that do not need to be prepared from the raw product state, but neither are they ready-to-serve. Examples of semi-prepared beverages are fruit cordials which only required the addition of water; iced coffee and cocktails may also be included in this category.

3. *Fully prepared beverages*: These are beverage products requiring virtually no preparation before being served to the customer, for example bottled fruit juices, spirits, wines

etc. In the majority of cases fully prepared beverages are majority of cases fully prepared beverages are dispensed in front of the customer, whether, for example, spirits at a bar or wines at a table.;

The style of beverage production in a catering operation should be complementary to the food production methods; therefore in high-class restaurant a full range of alcoholic and non-alcoholic beverages would be available. In a cafeteria operation, however, a limited range of beverages would be offered, and such non alcoholic beverages as tea, coffee or orange squash, may actually be 'prepared' by customers themselves, for example, by the use of a vending machine or a tea, coffee or soft drinks machine.

The beverage production method in a catering operation should be afforded the same importance and consideration as the choice of the food production method. Tea or coffee, for example, is often the last part of a customer's meal and reputations can be made or m erred on the taste of these beverages. Beverage production should also not be left to unskilled staff-this applies to the employees in the stillroom making the tea and coffee or the barmen mixing drinks and cocktails. The necessary requirements for good beverage production include the following: good quality raw materials-for example, a good blend of tea or coffee; the right equipments necessary for performing the job correctly-properly cleaned stills or machines, the provision of cock-tail shakers, strainers etc., if cocktails are being offered; and finally, the employees must be trained for the tasks they are to perform. The standard of beverage production in a catering establishment and the standards of hygiene and cleanliness in beverage equipment should be regularly checked. The method of beverage production must be such that it will operate within the financial limits, and meet the profit targets of the establishment, as laid down in the financial policy. Mismanagement in beverage production can have a substantial effect on the establishment's gross profit, in the same way as shortcomings in food production can, and for this reason must be afforded sufficient time, consideration and finance so that a suitable method of beverage production is chosen for the particular catering operation.

Quality Control in Food and Beverage Management

Quality Control

The food and beverage industry is a fast moving and exciting business. Looking at the Sunday papers, there are regular news articles about the expansion plans of new theme restaurants or multi-million pound take over deals; there are regular restaurant or hotel reviews and articles about cooking food at home. Television provides growing numbers of programmes on aspects of cookery from woks to barbecues, from cooking up a feast in twenty minutes to the real feasts of bygone eras. Cookery books, often tied to TV series, regularly top the bestseller lists. The food and beverage manager faces an increasingly knowledgeable and sophisticated customer with broader tastes and experiences than ever before. These customers demand satisfaction but are increasingly difficult to satisfy.

The customer translates these needs into a series of expectations of the service or product they will experience. If the restaurant meets or exceeds these expectations then the customer will feel satisfied and will feel that they have received 'quality'. If the restaurant does not meet their expectations, then there is a gap between customer expectations and the perceived characteristics of the service or product delivered to them and quality will not have been provided. It is implicit in this definition that quality can exist at any level of service, from fast food to fine dining, as long as expectations of that level of service are met.

The totality of features and characteristics that go to make up the meal experience are many and varied. They consist partly of the food itself, partly the service received and partly the environment created by the decor, furniture, lighting and music. One way of looking at these characteristics is to categorize them as relating to either the product or the service and as either tangible or intangible.

The tangible elements of the product are made up of the food on the plate and the items used to serve the food on or with. The designs of the crockery, cutlery and glassware as well as the table lay-up are all part of the meal experience. The menu provides evidence of the meal experience for the customer to see before purchase by displaying a verbal description or pictures of the dishes available. It is also important to consider how well the mechanical processes that a customer comes across in a food and beverage outlet operate. These include the speed and efficiency of the EFTPOS terminal as well as the way the vending machine dispenses a cup of hot chocolate.

The intangible elements of the product include the atmosphere of the operation and the aesthetic appeal of the decor, furniture and fittings. Every restaurant and bar has its own feel. Some are designed to be warm and friendly while others can be cold or clinical. Getting the decor right to give the customer the right feelings is obviously important.

The intangible elements of service are very hard to tie down but are easily experienced. A genuine smile brings with it warmth and friendliness. Some restaurants manage to find ways to let their customers know that staff care about their meal, but others only succeed in letting customers know that the staff care very little. These elements simply add up to a feeling of service and of being looked after.

Although service is thought of as intangible, there are elements that are tangible. Actions that service staff carries out during service are tangible. Speed of service can be measured: although customers' perceptions of time, especially if they are waiting for something, are often wrong. The ways of talking to customers that staff uses their scripts also provide hard evidence.

It is easiest for the food and beverage manager to control the tangible elements of the product and there is evidence that they are more important to the customer than the intangible elements of the product. On the other hand the intangible elements of service are probably more important to the customer than the tangible elements of service but they are much more difficult for any manager to influence. It is all well and good for an operation to meet customer requirements once, but it is no use to the customers if they receive exactly what they want on one day but, when the chef or their favourite crew member has a day off, the next visit is a disaster. The meaning of quality must also include reliability calls zero defects; this is the only acceptable quality standard. Across the organization, everyone should be striving to deliver to the customer right first time every time.

Some organizations are moving away from seeing quality as simply satisfying the customer and looking to 'delight' the customer by exceeding their expectations. If a customer is unhappy they will go to another supplier, but that a customer who is simply satisfied may also go somewhere else because they really have not got a lot to lose. The importance of repeat customers in generating profit, customers who tell everyone about how great their meal was and bring their friends with them next time are worth their weight in gold. There are however some dangers in trying to exceed customer expectations. It has been suggested that delight is the result of the added value of characteristics and features that customers did not expect arousing their latent expectations. Until a few years ago nobody expected their children to be given crayons and something to draw on when they went to a restaurant. Now it is almost commonplace. This highlights the problem of escalating expectations. Little extras soon become the expected norm and new 'delights' have to be found.

Quality in food and beverage operations means reliably providing the food, service and environment that meets with our customers' expectations and where possible finding ways of adding value to exceed expectations and result in delight.

There are three main sources of pressure on businesses to pay attention to quality.

First, customers are more demanding of every-thing they buy, as well as the way in which those products and services are delivered. Customers are no longer intimidated about complaining in restaurants and the trend to instruct service staff to check that all is well part way through the meal is asking for trouble.

Second, the development of more sophisticated hard and soft technologies allows managers to offer many possible additional and convenience services, although interpersonal contact is still seen as highly valued. The effectiveness of methods such as a good standard of dishes can be available from a vending machine and a microwave oven.

Lastly, in an increasingly competitive and international marketplace, quality is seen as providing an edge of competitive advantage.

Many managers, however feel that providing quality is too expensive or too much trouble to be of any real value an emphasis on quality brings three areas of benefits. The positive impact of quality on profit has been shown by the Profit Impact of Market Strategy (PIMS) study. In this study, the single most important factor affecting a business unit's performance is the quality of its products and services, in comparison to its competitors. A food and beverage operation that customers think has the quality edge over its competitors is able to boost profitability through charging premium prices. Quality provides leverage on the price/value relationship. Over the long term a quality advantage will result in business growth. This growth in volume will result in economies of scale and superior profit margins.

Providing high perceived value will lead to loyal customers, who will use the operation consistently over a long period and will recommend the unit to their friends. The value of long term relationships in services marketing has only recently been realized but good restaurateurs have always recognized the importance of repeat customers.

Quality improvement, without increasing the costs of an operation, results in operational efficiencies, which more than recoup the investment. Quality costs are divided into two the costs of conformance and the costs of non-conformance. The costs of conformance are the costs of assuring that everything comes out right and includes all efforts for prevention and quality education. The costs of non-conformance can be divided into appraisal/inspection costs and failure costs Appraisal costs are the costs of inspection to make sure that mistakes are kept down and to ensure that any mistakes that are made are identified before reaching the customer. Failure costs are the costs of having made mistakes. They are split into internal and external failure costs. Internal costs are those incurred where mistakes are found before they reach the customer or cross the line of visibility. They include scrap, rework, and downgrading and excess inventory. External failure costs are those incurred when mistakes are not found before they reach the customer. They include such things as repair and warranty claims, providing replacement goods or services and the potential loss of future business. External failure costs are much more serious than their internal counterparts because by the time the problem reaches the customer it is already too late. While the internal failure costs of excess inventory and waste might be high, the real danger of poor quality for a food and beverage operation lies in those errors that are not discovered until they reach the customer. Quality provides the opportunity for food and beverage operations to find a winning edge over their competitors, to ensure the long-term loyalty of their customers and to improve both short term and long-term profitability through cost savings and higher margins.

Managing Quality in Food and Beverage Operations

Increasingly, attention has been drawn to the service sector and the particular challenges faced by companies wishing to pursue service quality. Some tools and techniques have been adapted from manufacturing to cope with the challenges and, where necessary new approaches have been developed. Not only must food and beverage operations deal with the problems of manufacturing meals or drinks, they function also as a service operation. The resulting complexity makes managing quality in food and beverage operations more difficult but not impossible. Looking at the distinguishing characteristics of service operations provides some interesting insights for food and beverage operations.

Many services cannot be inspected or tested before sale because the production and consumption happen at the same time. It is not possible to test out an airline flight or a hair cut. On the production side of food and beverage operations, the range is from simultaneous production—such as in a hibachi restaurant where cooking is done in the restaurant to decoupled production such as cook-chill where food is batch produced at a central location, cooled, and then distributed for later consumption. There are, however, many other possible systems in between and each will have their own special requirements for quality management.

A restaurant seat is a perishable product. Empty places cannot be stockpiled for a busy day sometime in the future. Once a restaurant seat has been left empty, the revenue potential of that space is lost. On the product side, raw ingredients or complete meals can be stored for short periods depending on the method of storage. Food and beverage operations display many of the characteristics of service operations but they also have their own particular features. Providing a physical environment involves a substantial investment in premises and plant and associated fixed costs. Variable costs, however, are usually low. This cost structure means that generally the break-even volume will be quite high. Passing this volume will result in high profits, but low volumes will result in substantial losses. Making the most of capacity must be a high priority to the food and beverage manager. In itself this would not be a difficult challenge if forecasting demand levels were straightforward. However, demand tends to be complex and fluctuates over time, by type of customer and by menu item. The result is a mixture of patterns that makes the forecasting and scheduling of resources very difficult. Food and beverage production has a very short cycle of operation providing little time to monitor what is going on to correct any errors. A food and beverage operation can buy in fresh produce from the dawn markets that is prepared through the morning, on the menu for lunch and eaten by early afternoon.

When a customer enters an operation they place themselves in the care of the operation, which must employ all due diligence to ensure their safety. Food production processes deal with potentially contaminated raw ingredients with a limited shelf life. Poor handling can result in serious illness and death. The customer has very limited evidence of the hygiene standards of an operation upon which to make their choice of whom to trust. Recent developments in catering technology have allowed some decoupling of production and service with cook-chill, cook-freeze methods. The industrialized service delivery system of a fast food operation ensures high speed, high volume with high consistency over a limited product range and limited human intervention. These examples of technological substitution are unusual and still the emphasis is placed on the competence of the employees who produce and serve the food.

Faced with a complex operation the food and beverage manager is pressured by physical presence of the customer monitoring progress with the expert eye of someone who has eaten much news before. Even in home delivery operations the pressure of meeting the delivery times standard usually between 20-30 minutes.

Approaches to Quality Management

The importance of providing quality in any food and beverage operations there is a need for some form of systematic approach to quality. Quality and the consistency that should go with it will not happen by chance. It is the responsibility of the management to provide a frame work to encourage the delivery of quality it is the operative level staff who come face to face with customer and who produce the service or product the customer wants it is managers who insures that any barriers to quality are removed and the quality is improved

Quality Inspection

The earliest and easiest approach to quality is the inspection approach this simple approach is based on finding defects in a product or service before it reaches the customer by introducing and inspection by stages. Staff employed for that purpose if the problem is found the product will be rejected and sends back would probably carry out the taking. The inspection become something the staff dread. Quality is the question of checking physical attributes off against a checklist and hoping that nothing has been missed.

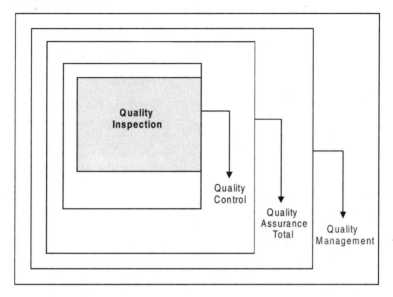

Quality Control

The quality control approach centers on inspection but recognizes the need of detailed specification and that quality checks should be made to out the production process. Quality control will not improve product or service quality it will only highlight when it has gone wrong. A non-conforming product or service must be produced before action can be taken to put it right and this leads to inefficiency and waste.

Quality Assurance

Quality assurance recognizes the inefficiencies of waiting for mistakes to happen and strives to design quality into the process so that things cannot go wrong or if they do they are identified and corrected as they happened. Lasting and continuous improvement in quality can be achieved through planning and preventing problems from arising at source. Moving the emphasis from inspection to prevention is helped by the introduction of a number of quality assurance tools and techniques such as statistical process control, blue printing and quality costing. The quality assurance involve the development of new operating philosophy and approach one that is proactive rather than reactive.

Total Quality Management

The focus on the customer and the scale and nature of internal and external environment are the main differences between the quality assurance and total quality management approaches in total quality management approach the driving force is the focus on the satisfaction of customer needs. The whole system must be directed as customer satisfaction and any thing that could get in the way of delivery this satisfaction must be removed. The emphasis is on a management led move towards teamwork and participation. Taking this holistic perspective can involve organization in significant changes in their culture. It may be relatively easy to introduce new systems and procedures but changing the cultures is much more difficult but necessary task.

Seven

Financial Aspects

Introduction

Today, with the continual increases in the costs of food, beverages, labour, energy, maintenance and other overheads, most establishments operate some form of budgetary control. A budget is a plan—expressed usually in financial and/or quantitative terms that reflects the policies of an establishment and determines the business operations for particular trading period. The trading period is usually of one year, but is often broken down into review periods of either thirteen four week periods; or alternatively, of thirteen week quarters, each quarter consisting of two four-week and one five-week periods. Which ever method is adopted it is necessary that the periods remain the same so as to make it possible to compare results not only with corresponding periods in the same year, but also with the corresponding periods in earlier years. Bank holidays and special events falling into different periods each year should be noted.

The term budgetary control refers to a method of control where particular responsibility for various budgeted results is assigned to the managers concerned and a continuous comparison of the actual results and budgeted figures is made. When there are discrepancies between the two, it is necessary identify the reasons for the variances and to cake appropriate action. It is essential that when budgets are set they are clearly seen to be achievable; otherwise they are of little value.

The objectives of budgetary control are three fold:

1. To provide a plan of action for a set trading period, to guide and regulate a business in keeping with its stated policies, and to maximize the full use of its resources.
2. To set standards of performance for management against which there performance can be measured.
3. To set out levels of cost responsibility and encourage cost awareness.

Budgets are prepared by the senior management of an organization in consultation with the various managers and departmental heads so as to ensure a greater level of commitment and an awareness of the aims, objectives, problems and possible weaknesses of the establishment.

Types of Budgets

Basically there are two main types:

(i) Capital budgets; and
(ii) Operating budgets.

Capital Budgets

Capital budget as the name implies, are those that are concerned with the assets and liabilities of an establishment, for example equipment, plant and cash.

Operating Budgets

Operating budgets are those' concerned with the day-to-day income and expenditure of an establishment and include sales, cost of sales, labour, maintenance, head office expenses, etc. It is shows as an example of the operating statement of a restaurant for a period in the trading year, together with the allocated budget targets for that period. The breakdown of the restaurant budget identifies further the specific standards of performance required of the restaurant management. When this is set against the recorded actual performance for that period the performance achieved can be measured. It is the usual practice to show not only the actual and budget information for a period but also the cumulative information for the year to date. The cumulative figures give a smoothing effect to any irregularities in performance of past periods as well as the overall picture of performance for the year so far.

The above budgets are prepared not only for each unit of a business, but also are broken down into budgets for departments such as individual restaurants, bars and banqueting. It is also common practice to consolidate the above budgets into a set of master budgets such as:

1. *A master budgeted trading account* for a particular trading period showing the predetermined volume of sales, the cost of sales and the gross profit expected.

2. *A master budgeted profit and loss account* for a particular trading period showing the predetermined income and expenditure and net profit expected. This highlights unit and departmental gross profits, labour costs, over-head costs and net profit.

3. *A master budgeted balance sheet* for a particular trading period showing the assets and liabilities at the beginning and at the end of the period.

Basic Stages in the Preparation of Budgets

For simplicity, budgeting may be seen as being in six stages. The amount of detail and sub division into departmental budgets depends very much on the type and size of the business. The basic stages are:

1. *Determination of the net profit* required for the business in relation to the capital invested and the risk involved. Alternatively, in the case of non-profit making establishments, the level of subsidy available or required is postulated.

2. *Preparation of the sales budget* this determines the volume of sales necessary to achieve the desired net profit or subsidy and also influences the budgeted costs for food, beverages, labour and some overheads.

3. *Preparation of administration and general budgets* these are for such items as head office expenses, advertising, rates, insurance, etc. Some of these may be regarded as fixed budgets, that is, they are not affected by any change in the volume of business, for example, head office expenses, advertising, rates, etc.; while others may be regarded as flexible budgets, that is, they are affected by changes in the volume of business, for example, telephones, laundry, etc.

4. *Preparation of the capital expenditure budget*, which makes provision for such items of expenditure as new kitchen equipment, restaurant and bar furniture including installation charges, etc.

5. *Preparation of the cash budget* this is regarded as the most important of the capital budgets and it predetermines the cash inflows, the cash outflows and resulting cash balance at particular points during the period.

6. *Preparation of master budgets* master budgets are prepared for the trading account, profit and loss account and the balance sheet.

Welfare Operations

The fact that food and beverage operations in the welfare sector for example, a hospital dining room or an employee restaurant may not be required to make a profit in the same way that commercial restaurants are, and that they may receive some form of subsidy, does not make budgeting any less necessary. When food and beverages are being sold at or near cost prices, or are being prepared within very strict subsidy cost limits, it is even more necessary that costs be estimated very accurately than where there is a large gross profit margin which can absorb some errors in costing. When the subsidy is for such items as heat, light, repairs, maintenance, furnishings, etc., control needs to be exercised on these expenses to keep them within the limits of the subsidy.

Costs, Profits and Sales

The cost of operating a catering unit or department is usually analyzed under the three headings of:

1. *Material costs*—cost of food and beverage consumed and the cost of additional items such as tobacco. The cost of any food and beverage provided to staff in the form of meals is deducted from material costs and added to labour costs. The food cost is then calculated by the formula:

   Opening stock + cost of purchases – closing stock – cost of staff meals = material cost

2. *Labour costs*—wages and salaries paid to all employees, plus any employer contribution to government taxes, bonuses, staff meals, pension fund, etc.
3. *Overhead costs*—all costs other than material and labour costs, for example rent, rates, insurance, depreciation, repairs, printing and stationery, china and glassware, capital equipment.

As most catering operations are subject to changes in the

volume of business done, it is normal practice to express the elements of cost and net profit as a percentage of sales. A change in the volume of sales has an effect on the cost structure and on the net profit.

Cost Groups

It is necessary to examine costs not only by their nature (material, labour, overheads) but also by their behaviour in relation to changes in the volume of sales. Using these criteria, costs may be identified as being of four kinds:

1. *Fixed costs*—These are costs, which remain fixed irrespective of the volume of sales, for example rent, rates, insurance, and the management element of labour costs.
2. *Semi-fixed costs*—These are costs, which move in sympathy with, but not in direct proportion to the volume of sales, for example fuel costs, telephone, laundry. Semis fixed costs contain a fixed and variable cost element.
3. *Variable costs*—These are costs, which vary in proportion to the volume of sales, for example food and beverage.
4. *Total costs*—This is the sum of the fixed costs, semi fixed costs and variable costs involved.

Profit

Three main kinds of profit are normally referred to in food and beverage operations:

1. *Gross profit* = total sales – cost of materials.
   The term gross profit is often referred to as 'kitchen profit' (food) or 'bar profit' (beverages). Room hire is normally treated as 100 per cent gross profit.
2. *After-wage profit* (or net margin) = total sales – (material + labour costs).

3. *Net profit* = total sales – total costs (material + labour +overhead costs).

All of the above are normally used as measures of performance against past results and budgeted targets.

Break-even Analysis

It is very common for food and beverage management to be faced with problems concerning the level of food and beverage cost that can be afforded, the prices that need to be set for food and beverages, the level of profit required at departmental and unit level and the number of customers required to cover specific costs or to make a certain level of profit.

Break-even analysis enables the relationship between fixed, semi fixed and variable costs at specific volumes of business to be conveniently represented on a graph. This enables the break-even point to be identified and the level of sales necessary to produce a predetermined level of net profit. The term break-even point may be defined as that volume of business at which the total costs are equal to the sales and where neither profit nor loss is made. The technique is based on the assumption that: the selling price remains constant irrespective of the volume of business; that certain unit costs remain the same over the sales range of the charted period; that only one product (for example, a meal) is being made or sold; that the product mix remains constant in cost price and volume and that labour and machine productivity is constant. Nearly every action or planned decision in a business will affect the costs, prices to be charged, the volume of business and the profit. Profits depend on the balance of the selling prices, the mix of products, the costs and the volume of business. The breakeven technique discloses the interplay of all these factors in a way, which aids food and beverage management in selecting the best course of action now and in the future.

Pricing is a multi-dimensional problem, which depends not only on the cost structure of a business and its specific profit objectives but also on the level of activity of the competition and the current business economic climate.

Pricing Considerations

The whole subject area of pricing is a complex one which unfortunately is not given the degree of priority that it requires. The pricing of a product has to meet the objectives of an organization and aspects related to pricing will normally be found in the financial, marketing and catering policies. For example, within the financial policy of a commercial organization, the basic aim of profit to be made in relation to the capital invested will be stated. The financial policy for an establishment in the welfare sector would state the level of subsidy to be allocated to the catering department and how it was to be calculated.

Quite naturally, the approach to pricing will differ, not only between the major sectors of the industry where normally in the non-commercial sector pricing is cost-orientated and in the commercial sector pricing is usually market-orientated but also between organizations within these sectors. For example, a fairly new growth-orientated organization could well be concerned with increasing its sales volume (and to do so may decide to keep its prices very competitive indeed) while an established organization may well be concerned with maintaining its net profit from an established sales volume.

Pricing Based on Cost

The traditional method used to establish the price of a menu item is to calculate, ideally from a standard recipe, the food cost per unit of the particular item and to add a given percentage of gross profit to arrive at the selling price. The percentage of gross profit applied should be sufficient to cover the fixed cost element (for example, rent, rates, etc., and payroll costs); the semi-fixed element (for example, heating, telephones, etc.); and a satisfactory element of net profit.

The advantages of this method are that it is quite easy to understand it and apply it.

The disadvantages of this cost plus method outweigh its advantages. First the relationship between the capital investment and net profit is ignored. The net profit achieved using the cost plus method is mainly related to the sales turnover in that the higher the volume of sales the higher will be the net profit achieved and vice versa. Second this method puts too much emphasis on the one element of cost that is the cost that is the cost of the ingredients of a food and beverage item on a menu and only generalizes on the fixed and semi fixed costs.

Lastly, this method is unrelated to the demands of the market place and is far too rigid to use as a method in the commercial sector of the industry.

Pricing Based on Market

The relationship between price and value for money is an important aspect of pricing. Value for money extends way beyond just the cost of the ingredients of the items chosen from a menu by a customer. The whole meal experience has to be taken into account, including such things as the atmosphere, decor, choice of menu items, level of service offered, etc. In order to be successful and to achieve a satisfactory volume of sales, pricing has to consider three basic factors:

Nature of the Demand for the Product

The economic concept of the elasticity of demand is relevant here. Elasticity of demand is the sensitivity of the sales volume to changes in price. A product would be said to have an elastic demand when a small decrease in the price charged would bring a significant increase in sales or, alternatively, if a small increase would bring about a significant decrease in sales. A typical example is changes in price of 10 per cent for products such as beer, named soft drinks, hamburgers, etc.

In the case of a product with an inelastic demand a small increase or decrease in price would not bring any significant increase or decrease in sales. A typical example might well be a change in price of 50p for products such as lobster, fillet steak, etc.; the customers who could afford these dishes would not be influenced by such a price change.

Level of the Demand for the Product

It is typical of most catering operations that they experience a fluctuating demand for their product not only hourly (e.g. as seen clearly in fast-food operations), but daily (e.g. in many hotel restaurants which on some days in the week have a low customer throughput). This fluctuation of demand normally affects their volume of sales and results in the underutilization of the premises, staff, etc., highlighting the necessity for a flexible approach to be given to pricing. This practice is commonly used in the industry and serves to increase the volume of sales even if the level of profitability may not be as great as under normal conditions. Typical examples of flexible pricing are 'bar-gain break' weekends; 'happy hours' in bars; a sliding scale for room hire for functions depending on the day of the week; etc.

Level of the Competition for the Product

Competition is a factor, as much as product cost and market demand, in determining selling prices. Competition exists from not only similar type operations but also from dissimilar operations—as in most instances customers are free to choose where they go and what amount they spend. Competition can include price, normally resulting in lower gross profit margins; or quality of food, service, decor, etc. normally resulting in higher gross profit margins.

Menu Pricing

Departmental Profit Margins

The approach to menu pricing must follow from the outline of the basic policies and from the determined departmental profit targets. Each department will have a significant role in the total organization and its individual profit tar-gets will normally be unrelated. For example, in a hotel the profit required from the a la carte restaurant may well be far lower than that of its coffee shop. The existence of the a la carte restaurant may be mainly of an image status for the hotel as against being a major profit contributor. What is necessary is for the total sum of the individual departments' contributions to equal the desired contribution to the revenue for the whole establishment.

Differential Profit Margins

It is unusual to apply a uniform rate of gross profit to all of the items found on a food menu or beverage list, although this simplistic method of costing can at times still be found in the non commercial sector of the industry. In the non-commercial sector of the industry one of the advantages is that where a uniform rate of gross profit is applied (for example, 60 per cent), reference to the takings can quickly show the costs at 40 per cent gross profit irrespective of the sales mix and an immediate comparison can be made to the actual usage of materials. The reasons for not applying a uniform rate of gross profit in the commercial sector are those already stated earlier in this chapter, that is, it ignores such things as capital investment; it emphasizes the cost too much; it ignores competition; etc. Further, it could distort the range of prices and values of items on a menu in that a low food/beverage cost item would end up being priced at a very low price, while a high food/beverage cost item would be exorbitantly priced. In addition, it does not allow any flexible approach to the selling of items. Differential profit margins take into account the sales mix of items from a food menu or beverage list and hopefully provide the competitive balance of prices so that in total it is attractive to the customer and achieves the desired gross profit and revenue for the department.

Special Pricing Considerations

Sales Tax

Depending on the government in power, it is likely that some form of sales tax may be enforced during its period of office. It is important to the customer to know whether prices displayed or quoted are inclusive of this sales tax or not. Additionally, the caterer needs to realize that any money collected on behalf of the government has at some time to be paid to that government and that it should not be included when calculating revenue or average spend figures, etc.

Service Charge

This is an additional charge, made to customers, at a fixed percentage of the total cost of the food and beverage served. The fixed percentage is determined by management, printed on the menu/beverage list, with the objective of removing from the customer the problem of determining what size of tip to give when in a particular establishment. As this charge is to be distributed to the staff at a later date, usually on a points system, it should be treated similarly to a sales tax and not included in the calculation of revenue for food and beverages or in the calculations of average spend figures.

Cover Charge

This is an additional charge to a meal in restaurants to cover such costs as the bread roll and butter and items included but not priced on a menu. Care should be exercised as to whether to implement this or not as it is most likely to cause aggravation to some clients when it is applied.

Minimum Charge: restaurants to discourage some potential clients from using the premises and to discourage clients from taking up a seat and only purchasing a very low-priced item.

Menu Pricing Application

The exact method of pricing used by an establishment will depend on such matters as which sector of the industry the establishment is in; the level of profit/subsidy required; its basic policies; etc. It is important though to remember that the price in itself can be a valuable selling tool and a great aid in achieving the desired volume of sales.

Table d'hote Menus

This type of menu is characterized by being a restricted menu, offering a small range of courses with a limited choice within each course and at a fixed selling price. The price may be just one price for any three courses chosen, or may vary in price depending on the main course chosen. The method of pricing chosen should take into account the departmental profit required and the differential profit margins of the menu. Based on the forecasted sales take-up by guests, the *average* should be taken to fix the price. The average may well be the true figure, rounded off, when the objective is to attract as many customers as possible to choose from the menu; or alternatively, it may be an *average plus* figure when it is being offered with an a la carte menu and it is not desired to encourage too many guests away from the a la carte menu by making the price differentiation too attractive.

A la Carte Menus

This type of menu is characterized by being a larger menu than a table d'hote menu offering a greater choice of courses and dishes within each course, and each item being individually priced. The method of pricing here is again to take into account the departmental profit required and the differential profit margins for each course and then to price each item separately using standard recipes. In addition, note should be taken of the potential sales mix within each course so as to achieve the desired profit margin.

Banqueting Menus

This is a specific type of table d'hote menu offering normally no choice to the customers. The specific difference in pricing this menu is that apart from the food and often the liquor, all the additional items are normally priced and charged separately. Examples of such items are flowers for each table, a band, meals and refreshments for the band, services of a toast master, hire of a microphone, printing of a special menu for the function. The pricing of a banquet menu for a client is commonly found to have a flexible element to it, in that it is not uncommon for a banqueting manager to offer additions to a menu at no additional cost to the client in order to obtain the business during a slack trading period or for a particular gap in a week. For example, the banqueting manager may offer as a free addition to the standard printed menu such things as a soup course, a sorbet etc. Further, the charge for the hire of the function room may be reduced or removed altogether.

Pricing of Beverages

The method used to price beverages is similar to that for pricing foods. As in the case of foods, first, the departmental profit target and gross profit percentage should be set, followed by differential profit margins based on the sales mix achievable. The sales mix breakdown depends on the type of operation and how detailed the breakdown of sales is required. The gross profit percentage of house brand beverages that is, the particular brand of beverage that is offered to the customer, when a specific brand is not requested is usually higher than on other brand beverages as it is normally made available by the supplier at a special discounted rate. Pricing may be more accurately calculated for beverages as little, if any, processing of the drinks takes place drinks being purchased by the bottle (for example, beer, wine) or by a specific stated measure (for example, 6-out) from a bottle of known standard size (for example, wine, 75 cl). The mixing of drinks is, like food, usually prepared using a standard recipe particular to an establishment.

Subsidized Operations

There are many operations within the non-commercial sector of the industry that are subsidized in some form or other. Subsidies may take the form of completely free premises, capital equipment, services and labour or the catering department may be required pay a percentage of these costs with the balance being the subsidy. Pricing in this situation may, for example, require the sales revenue to cover the food costs only; or food costs plus specific named expenses (for example, all labour); or food costs plus a named percentage (for example, 20 per cent) as a contribution to all overheads. Pricing in this situation is frequently done on a cost-plus basis, depending on the level of subsidy. When more than the food/beverage cost has to be recovered, it is important that prices are competitive enough to encourage a high enough volume of sales.

Profit Improvement

Maintaining and improving an adequate level of profit are essential for all businesses today to survive particularly with the increasing level of competition tempting customers not only to change from their usual type of restaurant, but also from the many other types of leisure businesses all chasing the same customers' restricted amount of disposable income. Among the problems often facing the food and beverage manager is how can the profitability be maintained or increased. Should the prices for some or all items be increased and by how much, and/or food and beverage items costs be reduced, and/or labour costs reduced, and/or the number of customers increased, etc.

Two accepted methods of profit improvement are profit sensitivity analysis and menu engineering.

Profit Sensitivity Analysis

PSA is concerned with identifying the 'critical' or 'key factors' (i.e. the determinants of profitability) of a business and establishing how they rank in influencing its net profit. The emphasis of PSA is on net profit and the examination of that area that responded positively to change. In order to undertake PSA the 'profit multipliers' of the business must firstly be calculated.

The method is:

1. Identify the 'key factors', financial and operational of the business.
2. Assume a change in one 'key factor' at a time of say 10 per cent, whilst holding all others constant.
3. Calculate the resulting change in net profit.

4. Calculate the profit multipliers (PM):

PM = per cent change in net profit/per cent change in 'key factors'

5. List the PMs in order of size.
6. Analyze the results.

Menu Engineering

Plow Horses	Stars
Customer perception:	Customer perception:
Over-priced, standard-type items	Restaurant's prestige items
Management action:	Price unimportant to purchase decision
	Management action:
■ Ensure rigid specifications for purchasing, recipe and presentation are strictly maintained.	■ Ensure rigid specifications for purchasing, recipe and presentation are strictly maintained.
■ Locate items to a low profile position on menu.	■ Feature prominently on menu.
■ To increase contribution margin by 'packaging' with a high contribution item.	■ Regularly promote.
■ Test small price increases.	■ Test price increases in 'high season.'
Dogs	**Puzzle**
Customer perception:	Customer perception:
Low-priced, but items dull and uninteresting.	Tempting but overpriced
Management action	Management action
■ Try revamping item.	■ Reposition and facture more prominently on menu.
■ If a new menu item, spend time to check if it can be improved.	■ Increase merchandising.
■ Review alternative menu items.	■ Re-name item and change the presentation.
■ Increase the price and raise status to 'puzzle'.	■ Give the item 'special' status.
■ Remove from menu.	

Menu engineering is a marketing orientated approach to the evaluation of a menu with regard to its present and future content, design and pricing. Its origins are based on the famous Boston Consulting Group (BCG) portfolio technique, a matrix specifically designed to analyze individual business performance in a company with a range of different business interests. The concept of menu engineering requires food and beverage managers to orient themselves to the contribution that menu items make to the total profitability of a menu. It highlights the good and the poor performers in a menu, and provides vital information for making the next menu more interesting and appealing to the customers, and hopefully more profitable. Menu engineering is a step-by-step procedure that focuses on thebe three main elements:

1. *Customer demand*—the number of customers served;
2. *Menu mix*—an analysis of customer preferences for each menu item (popularity);
3. *Contribution margin*—an analysis of the contribution margin (GP%) for each menu item.

The prerequisites to using this technique are:

1. The standardization of all recipes (including the presentation), so that the food costs can be accurate;
2. The accurate sales analysis of each menu item, daily and by meal period;
3. The use of a personal computer, so that simple spreadsheets, with standard calculations, may be done accurately and with speed.

Using the simple matrix, menu items can be plotted, representing their performance with regard to volume (popularity) and cash contribution (profit). The four squares of the matrix commonly have names indicating the performance of items in a particular square.

1. *Star*—Menu items high in menu mix (popularity) and also high in contribution margin

2. *Plowhorses*—Menu items high in menu mix (popularity) but low in contribution margin.
3. *Puzzles*—Menu items low in menu mix (popularity) and high in contribution margin.
4. *Dogs*—Menu items low in menu mix and low in contribution margin.

The analysis of the data to understand menu engineering is done using a standard computer spreadsheet package. This takes the form of a large grid compromising of rows and columns where labels, formulae and values can be entered. When in operation the formulae and values can be changed if required giving instaneous calculations of the figures and hard copies printed and retained for easy reference. Whilst spreadsheet can be complied by hand the time taken would be lengthy and the opportunity to frequently undertake what if exercise less likely. It should be noted that the success in being able to move menu items up the matrix to the status of a star could have an undesirable effect on the profitability of the menu simply because customers do not always of the food and beverage manager.

Eight

Advertising, Public Relations, Merchandising and Sales Promotion

Advertising

Advertising is concerned with contacting and informing a market of an operation's product, away from the point of sale and is involved with influencing the customers' behaviour and attitude to the product before they enter the service operation. The American Marketing Association as has defined advertising: Any paid form of non-personal presentation and promotion of ideas, goods or services by an identified sponsor. Its purpose, as defined by the Institute of Practitioners in Advertising (IPA) is to influence a person's knowledge, attitude and behaviour in such a way as to meet the objectives of the advertiser.

The aims and objectives of an operation's advertising policy should be contained within the marketing plan. No advertising campaign ought to be undertaken unless it has been properly organized and is going to be efficiently managed. Disorganized advertising will not benefit an establishment; it may, in fact, do a great deal of harm. It is, therefore, wrong to assume that any advertising is better than no advertising.

The size of a food services advertising budget is dependent on a number of factors:

1. Nature of the catering operation, whether it is in the commercial or non-commercial sector.
2. Size of the operation the larger the commercial operation, the larger the advertising budget available
3. Ownership of the catering facility In a small, privately owned hotel or restaurant, the responsibility for advertising may be in the hands of the owner or manager. In a large multi-unit organization, the responsibility for advertising is either assigned to a specialist department within the organization, or given to a professional outside advertising agency.
4. The number and nature of the market segments being aimed at.
5. The amount of advertising each market segment requires to be adequately covered.
6. The type of advertising to be used. Peak time national television coverage will obviously cost considerably more than a local radio broadcast. In some sectors of the industry advertising budgets are very large.

Generally speaking, advertising expenditure in this sector of the industry varies from 0.5 to 4.5 per cent turnover. Companies within the hotel industry are also increasing their advertising budges considerably. Where small owner-managed or small groups of hotels cannot afford to individually advertise their properties and facilities to any great effect, they may group together to form a marketing consortium to achieve greater advertising impact. By joining together with other small or similar operations, an individual establishment benefits from being part of a large organization. Whatever the size of the food service facility, however, advertising does have relevance and importance. In order to be effective, there must be a clear understanding of the purposes and objectives of advertising. In a catering operation these would include the following:

1. *To create awareness of the product*: Making the maximum number of customers aware of an operation's products, utilizing the tools of advertising available to that particular operation.

2. *To create desire for the product*: Customers purchase a product because of the benefits they feel they will gain from that product. Advertising, therefore, needs to create a desire for an operation's product by stressing customer benefits. The benefits of take away meals, for example, are that raw ingredients do not have to be purchased, stored, pre-pared and cooked. The end product is ready to eat, time is saved and cleaning up after-wards is minimal. These are some of the benefits that customers perceive as important when they buy a take-away meal, they are not just buying food for physiological needs.

3. *To influence customer's attitudes to the product*: This may be in the short or long term.Over a number of years, for example, an organization may wish to portray a 'caring' image towards its customers. It may choose to do this by using repetitive advertising reinforcing its caring attitude.

4. *To create brand loyalty*: In order to do this, a successful brand image must be created by the company, so that when customers consider buying a certain type of meal, they immediately think of a certain restaurant or fast-food operation.

5. *To persuade customers to buy*: This will only be achieved if the advertising campaign has been directed at the appropriate level of the market. For example, if an

advertising campaign incorrectly portrays an average priced restaurant as being an expensive place to eat, customers with a lower average spending power will not choose to visit the facility because of the high-priced image portrayed; equally, customers with a high average spending power may be disappointed with their choice of restaurant. The operation's target markets must, therefore, be divided into clearly identifiable market segments. The promotional features of the marketing side can then be aimed specifically at these market segments.

6. To persuade customers to visit an operation in preference to a competitor's. Competition may be direct or indirect. Direct competition includes those operations competing for the same target market.

7. *To remind customers to buy*: The objectives of an advertising campaign alter during the life cycle of the product. For example, in the introductory phase of a product launch, creating awareness for first-time buyers is an important objective of advertising. When the product enters its growth and maturity stages and the company is heavily reliant on repeat purchases, the main objective of the advertising campaign may then shift to reminding existing and past customers to buy. This is equally applicable to operations within both the commercial and non-commercial sectors. It has particular reference in situations such as the work place where catering facilities are usually in the same block of offices or factory, and where staff may become accustomed to passing by the catering facilities and perhaps choosing to eat elsewhere. An advertising campaign to attract and remind this market segment is a particularly effective way of building up repeat business.

8. *To inform the market about a product*: For example, some fast-food chains now produce nutritional guides about their products that are available to customers of their restaurant

and take-away outlets.

9. To provide reassurance about the product. This is particularly relevant in the catering industry where a customer often leaves a restaurant without any tangible evidence of a purchase. Customers' worries and anxieties about a product need to be allayed so that they feel they made a good purchase and will, therefore, feel disposed to make another. In the example of the nutritional guides, as well as being informative, they also reassure customers that the meals they are buying are nutritionally sound. This is particularly important with the current interest in healthy eating and diets.

10. From an ethical point of view, the operation's advertising must portray a truthful picture of the establishment. Customers may quite rightfully be disillusioned and annoyed if they read that a particular restaurant is offering a free glass of wine to every customer, or features some specialty drinks, only to arrive and find that the establishment has 'run out' or 'sold out' of these items. The following advertising techniques are all applicable in some way to both commercial and non-commercial operations. However, depending largely on the sector of the industry and the size of the advertising budget available, the larger commercial organizations are able to utilize many or all of these advertising tools, whereas smaller non-commercial operations will be restricted to only a few.

The major forms of advertising that may be employed by food service facilities include the following:

Direct Mail

Involves communicating by post to specified customers; it may be directed at new and potential customers or to past or well-established customers. It involves the direct mailing of personalized

pes of magazines in which a catering operation
advertise include professional journals and
siness management magazines and the 'social'
which are read by particular target market groups.
of advertising in specific magazines are that
e measured; they have a longer 'shelf life' than
may be re-reading many times.

nber of 'Good Food Guides' produced in which
cilities may wish to be included. To be featured
will often be as a result of passing a professional
he particular organization and at times having to
clusion. As a method of advertising these guides
alue in that they all have large circulation figures
sed by interested and potential customers and are
as sources of reference for eating out occasions.

sing

lesale' advertising is the selling of an operation's
ies through 'middle men' such as travel agents,
perators, etc. At present it is mainly the large hotel
aurant chains that have utilized this form of external
h it is also available to small restaurants that are
d. By approaching local tour operators, for example,
aurant may be able to secure a regular weekend
e of between twenty and thirty covers throughout
nonths. Such an arrangement not only has the
ncreased sales for the operation, but also aids in the
enus, food costing, staffing levels, etc., for several
ance. These middlemen for the provision of their
e a commission fee; this may vary between 5 and

letters, brochures, pamphlets and leaflets, and as a form of
advertising offers a number of advantages:

1. Specific customer can be targeted. For example members
   of a specific profession within a defined area, member of
   a particular club or society, residents on a housing estate,
   etc. Repeat business in particular can develop by mailing
   personalized birthday, anniversary and Christmas cards,
   details of special promotions, events and offers to regular
   and occasional customers.
2. Direct mail is easy to introduce. It can either be initiated
   by the organization itself by producing its own mailing
   lists, or an external mail service agency or list broker
   may be used. It can be used by both small and large
   operations.
3. The feedback from targeted customers is relatively prompt
   and easy to appraise. Free post return cards, free phone
   telephone calls are usually returned soon after the direct
   mail shot has been received, or not at all. The use of
   coupons, vouchers etc. is easy to appraise in that they are
   normally only for use in a restricted period and the uptake
   can be measured easily.
4. It is a cost-effective method of advertising to specifically
   targeted groups of customers with very little 'wastage'.

However, direct mail also has a number of disadvantages:

1. The market must be specifically targeted or the mail shots
   are a complete waste of money.
2. The mail must be received, read and acted upon by the
   specific individual or group or all prior advertising
   research has also been a waste.
3. The production of good-quality mailing literature can be
   costly. Personalized letters should ideally be used as
   duplicated material has little impact and is often discarded

straight away. The envelope too must encourage the recipient to open it rather than discarding it as a circular. Once the initial mail has been sent out, careful monitoring of subsequent replies is necessary; often further advertising material may need to be distributed to reinforce the initial sales literature.

The identification of the market segments to be aimed at is most important. As with marketing research, the operation may find that through its own desk research internal and external it can amass a considerable amount of information about its markets through restaurant reservations, sales records, trade journals, local newspapers, etc. If a restaurant is considering featuring special business lunches, for example, it may consider writing to civic and business associations and asking for their membership lists, as well as contacting any other professional groups in the area. Alternatively, a catering operation may consider using a professional mail service agency. Here again, it is important to specify exactly the section of the market to be aimed at. Large catering organizations that have sufficient finance available are able to deal directly with advertising agencies that will totally man-age an organization's advertising campaign. They will study the product to be marketed, design appropriate advertisements, and suggest possible outlets for distributing these adverts, whether through the press, on posters, direct mailing or whatever.

For the smaller organization, however, the use of a professional advertising agency for all the operation's requirements is not always feasible because of the costs involved. For the smaller organization with a limited advertising budget it may be more advantageous to identify where in the advertising campaign the operation would most benefit from professional advice and to seek this advice when necessary. The operator may decide, for example, that the two most effective ways of reaching potential markets are direct mailing and advertising in

the local newspape
advertising and the ti
of the advertisement
stage even the small
help and advice of a
an advertisement in
local newspaper, or t
restaurant brochure ar
piece of sales literature
and existing customer
of a catering operatio
portray. Therefore e
allocation to Advertisi
of this can be well
professional designer
literature for the cateri

Press Advertising

Newspaper

Advertising in national
probably one of the most
operations. Because re
featured together in a ne
an advertisement featurir
will stand apart from the
direct mailing, advertisin
and organized. If an adver
records must be kept of tho
to the advertisement and w
segments originally aime
informing a basis for plan

Magazines

The different t
may choose t
publications, b
type magazines
The advantage
response may
newspapers an

Guides

There are a nu
food service f
in these guides
inspection by
pay a fee for i
have a special
and are purch
used regularly

Trade Advert

Trade or 'who
catering facil
package tour
groups and res
selling althou
privately own
a country res
lunchtime tra
the summer
advantage of
planning of r
months in ad
services cha

12.5 percent depending on what functions and services they have provided for the catering operation.

Broadcasting

Radio

Advertising on commercial radio is mainly limited to local radio stations that broadcast within a specific radius. It may be used to advertise local take-away, restaurants, and hotels, wine bars etc. Its main advantages are that it is a very up-to-date form of advertising, not too costly and has the potential to reach a large percentage of local custom people at work, driving cars, using personal stereos, people at home, etc.

Televisions

Television's major advantage over radio is its visual impact. Its major disadvantage is its high cost, particularly during peak receiving times. Its national use is limited almost exclusively to the larger restaurant and fast food and popular restaurant chains and hotel groups. Some regional television advertising may be undertaken but at present is very limited. The use of both videocassette recorders and cable television are two further extensions of TV and their use in private homes, clubs, hotels, shopping malls etc. is increasing annually.

Cinemas

Cinema advertising is also highly visual but also very localized. Catering facilities such as fast food and popular restaurants etc. open until late in the evening are often featured, but are usually quite specific to a certain area.

Signs and Posters

Signs and posters advertising a catering facility may be positioned either very close to it or some distance away. They are used along streets in towns and cities on hoardings, in airport lounges, railway carriages and the underground subways. External signs on main roads are particularly important for hotels, restaurants and fast-food drive-in operations who rely heavily on transient trade, and it is, therefore, important for these advertisements to be easily read and their messages understood quickly. Traffic traveling at high speeds must also be given adequate time to pull in. Posters displayed in the street, in railway carriages etc. can afford to be more detailed because passengers and passersby will have more time available to read them. As with all other forms of advertising, signs and posters must portray the type of image the restaurant is trying to achieve. Fast food and take-away outlets in high street locations, for example, which are attempting to attract as much transient traffic as possible, feature large colourful signs with distinguishing logos and colours. An up-market restaurant situated outside a town, however, would not need to use such obvious external signs, because a higher percentage of the trade would already have made a reservation and such a restaurant would, therefore, display something smaller and more discreet.

Miscellaneous Advertising Media

This includes other forms of advertising media that may be used in addition to the major channels discussed above. For example, door-to-door leaflet distributions, leisure centre entrance tickets, theatre programmes, shop windows etc.

Public Relations

Public relations is a communication and information process, either personal or non personal, operating within an organization's internal and external environment. It involves the creation of a favourable environment in which an organization can operate to the best of its advantage. An organization would typically be involved internally in communicating to its customers and employees, and eventually to its customers, suppliers, sales force, local community, council and government departments, etc. Public relations has two main functions:

1. It has a problem-solving or trouble-shooting function to deal with any negative publicity. As with advertising, it is wrong to assume that any publicity is better than no publicity. Detrimental newspaper reports and letters to column writers, bad word-of-mouth and radio news publicity can all have a damaging effect on an operation's image and sales. Through a public relations exercise a company's desired corporate image can be restored.

2. It has a forward-looking function to creating positive publicity for the organization and may be used at various stages during the life cycle of the facility. For example, if a fast food unit is to be opened in a busy town center, a public relations exercise would typically be to create a favourable environment and attitude within the local community before its opening. If this facility were specifically aiming at a younger family market, the public relations function would include informing the identified market segments of the benefits the facility has to offer to them. For example children's menus and portions will be available at reduced prices, high chairs for babies are to be provided, an informal atmosphere will exist, on certain days entertainment for the children will be organized, a young members' club will be available for those wishing to join etc. In institutional catering, the role of public relations may be to explain to a staff committee the need for certain price increases to be passed on to the staff cafeteria, or why different products have been bought to replace existing ones etc. The initiation of a public relations exercise should begin with the identification of that sector of the organization's environment that it wishes to

communicate with; it may, for example, be a particular segment of its market, the press, local schools etc. An evaluation of the organization's existing corporate image with that sector will highlight those areas it feels are unfavourable, and would benefit from a public relations exercise. The organization may then choose the most suitable channels for communicating its messages to help create the type of environmental climate it feels would be favourable to its own company's objectives.

The choice of public relations tools to be used depends largely on the target audience, the suitability of one media over another and the budget available.

They would include:

1. *Press media*—Newspapers, magazines, trade journals, brochures, leaflets, guides, press conferences, press releases.
2. *Broadcasting media*—Television, radio, cinema, promotional video and cassettes
3. *Community media*—Sponsorship of local events, individuals, companies, exhibitions, talks, free gifts, samples.

Depending on the size of the organization, the public relations function may be the responsibility of the owner, or manager, it may be an individual's task in a medium-sized operation, a separate department within the organization consisting of a number of employees, or an external public relations company may be used. Public relations in the hotel and catering industry has a real application whether the catering facility is a small or large operation, is independent or part of a large group, exists in the free market or captive. The importance of public relations is the ability to communicate and inform. The public image, good or bad, of a catering facility is something that develops as a result of the business activity; however, whether it is advantageous or disadvantageous to the organization can be greatly influenced by public relations advertise special events, forthcoming attractions, etc. In these areas in hotels, restaurants and clubs, people may be waiting in a queue or for the arrival of other guests, and therefore have the time to read the notices on these stands. In the work place they can be placed in areas with a high throughput of pedestrian traffic, for example in corridors, and in general locations where people congregate such as beside vending machines. The announcements on these stands must be kept attractive and up to date or the messages grow old and ineffective. Some self-service operations use floor stands at the head of the waiting line to show the menu in advance and selected specialties of the day.

Merchandising

The merchandising of catering operations involves the point of sale promotion of their facilities using non-personal media. Unlike advertising it is not a paid for form of communication, but like sales promotion is more concerned with influencing customer behaviour in the short term. Once customers are inside a restaurant they have already made their decision as to the type of establishment they wish to eat in; their subsequent decisions are concerned with what particular aspects of the product they will now choose. Customers may decide to eat at a restaurant because they have seen it advertised, and will therefore bring to the restaurant-preconceived ideas as to the standard of food, level of service etc., that they will receive. It is important at this stage that the point of sale merchandising of the restaurant should support its advertising campaign in order to achieve a sense of consistency and totality. For example, if the restaurant has been advertising specialty dishes for a particular week, these must be available when the customer arrives at the restaurant. The major types of merchandising that may be employed by a catering operation include the following:

Floor Stands

Floor stands or bulletin boards are particularly effective if used in waiting and reception areas to:

Posters

Posters have a wider circulation than the previously described floor stands. They may be displayed in reception areas, elevators, and cloakrooms, in the restaurant dining area itself; in fact they may be placed in any strategic positions where people have the time available to read their messages. Consideration must not only be given to the area in which these advertisements should be placed, but also their positions within these areas. In elevators, for example, they are often placed at the back when the majority of people face forwards or look upwards as soon as they enter a lift and therefore only give a poster at the back a momentary glance. Similar thought should be given to the position of posters in reception areas; for example, their height should be at eye level and they need to be placed away from the entrance and exit doors that people tend to pass through quickly.

Wall Displays

Illuminated wall displays are used extensively by fast-food operations showing enlarged colour photographs of the food and beverages available. They are also used by wine bars, cocktail bars and lounges and look particularly attractive at night. Blackboards are often found in pubs, bars, school cafeterias and theme restaurants where the dish of the day and other specials can be changed regularly along with their prices.

Tent Cards

Tent cards are often placed on restaurant dining tables to promote special events, attractions, etc. are valuable merchandising tool because guests will almost inevitably pick the card up and read it at some point during the meal, and they may even take it away with them. They may be used to advertise special dishes or wines, or announce forthcoming events such as New Year Party. Again, these cards should be changed regularly to hold interest and must always be up to date and clean. In hotels or other operations that have a variety of catering outlets, these tent cards are very useful in advertising the other facilities within the same establishment. In a cocktail bar, for example, tent cards may be used to advertise the a la carte restaurant, and in the restaurant the customers' attention may be drawn to special function arrangements the operation offers. This type of merchandising can help to make customers aware of the operation's alternative facilities and hence boost sales in these areas.

Clip-on

Menu clip-on are most commonly used in restaurants to advertise specialty items, plats du jour, special table d'hote lunches offered in an a la carte restaurant and so on; they may also be used on wine lists to promote a particular wine or region. Both tent cards and clip-on are useful tools for the hotel or restaurant to feature the higher profit earning food and beverage items. 'Loss leaders' may be placed towards the end of the menu selection.

Children's Menus

Children's menus and portion sizes are particularly applicable to those catering operations that attract family custom, for example resort hotels, fast-food units, medium-priced restaurants etc. Some restaurants offer a reduced price for children's portion sizes while others produce a separate children's menu, which also contains games and puzzles to keep the children occupied while the parents are having their meal. This is particularly applicable to those operations that rely heavily on family trade, and even if children's menus are not offered throughout the year, they maybe worthwhile considering during the busier summer months.

Visual Food and Beverage Display

It was once said that 'We eat with our eyes' and in few other situations could this be truer than in the actual cooking and presentation of the food to the customer. Visual selling in a catering operation can be enhanced by the use of several techniques:

Display

A good display of well-presented food can do much to increase sales. Impulse buying is the purchasing of a product at a point of sale on the strength of its visual presentation, with little or no preconceived thoughts of buying that product. Good displays are necessary in any situation; customers may be encouraged to purchase more when they actually see the food and beverages, for example at self-service restaurants, buffets, carvery operations and vending machines.

Trolleys or Carts

The use of trolleys or carts is another method of selling food and beverages by using display techniques. In a restaurant there may be a variety of trolleys used for hors d'oeuvres, desserts, hot and cold meat joints, liqueurs and cigars.

Gueridon Cookery

A gueridon trolley in a restaurant may be used for finishing off a particular dish before being presented to the customer, or it may be used to cook a complete dish, for example flam be desserts. This particular type of action presentation often encourages other guests in the restaurant to also try these types of dishes.

Other Display Cookery

Some operations deliberately open up their kitchens so that customers can see their food being cooked, for example steak houses where steaks are openly grilled on a charcoal grill, and other operations which roast poultry and other meat on rotating spits. In these types of operation special attention must be given to the balance between this type of display cookery and the other items on the menu to ensure that any additional expenses, such as staffing and food costs, are justified by the increase in custom.

Beverage Display

The display of beverages, alcoholic and non-alcoholic, cans also con-tribute to impulse purchases, rather than being just a single coffee sale at the end of a meal. In a self-service cafeteria bottles and glasses of cooled fruit juices, and wine can all look inviting; in a restaurant, full wine racks, or full bottles at the side of the buffet or carvery table have a similar visual effect.

Audio

Audio merchandising has fairly limited application, but can be used in situations with a 'captive' audience, for example to promote a coffee shop, pizza bar, ice-cream parlour in a shopping mall, to focus attention on a hospital's cafeteria via the hospital radio, to inform exhibition visitors in a conference center of the catering facilities available.

Other Sales Tools

There are a variety of other internal sales tools that may be used by a catering operation. These include place mats, which in coffee shops may contain the breakfast menu with a reminder that the operation is open throughout the day for snacks; napkins; doilies; and pre-portioned condiments which all add to the operation's sales message. In the bars giving away cocktail sticks, matches and drink mats also enables a small part of the operation to be carried out of the establishment and may act as a reminder to customers of their meal experience several days or months later. Small part of the operation to be carried out of the establishment and may act as a reminder to customers of their meal experience several days or months later.

Through all aspects of an organization's merchandising approach, there is a very real need for it to complement its advertising campaign. Advertising the facilities will hopefully have stimulated customer interest. The role of merchandising is to convert that interest into purchases and increased sales.

Sales Promotion

Sales promotion is a form of temporary incentive highlighting aspects of a product that are not inherent to it. Sales promotion may be aimed at customers, distribution channels and sales employees. It does not necessarily occur at the point of sale, although in many instances it does. Sales promotion is used by operations for a number of reasons including the following:

1. To increase the average spends by customers and thereby increases the sales revenue.
2. To promote a new product or range of products being featured by the operation, for example offering a new flavoured milk shake in a take-away facility at a reduced price.
3. To influence impulse purchasers towards a certain product or range of products, for example featuring Australian wine at a special discount price.
4. To aid as a reminder during a long-term advertising campaign, for example on long established main menu items.
5. To help 'level' peak activities of business, for example offering a free glass of wine to customers ordering their meal before 18.30 hours.
6. To celebrate a special event.

7. To 'package' together menu items at an attractive price, for example steak and strawberries. Such 'packages' are seasonal in nature but aid in directing a high proportion of customers' choices towards items of a low preparation labour content.
8. To clear slow moving stock, for example pricing specific cocktails at two for the price of one.

The targets being aimed at influence the types of sales promotions used:

Customer
Sales promotions aimed directly at customers include money-off coupons, discounts or special prices during off-peak periods, free chicken meals for families, a free bottle of wine for every two adult meals ordered etc. Special events and promotions may be communicated to the customer by advertising, by direct mail, by telephone or by posters and tent cards.

Distribution Channels
Promotional techniques aimed at incentivating third party agents include free restaurant meals, free gifts, com-petitions and the use of the hotel's leisure facilities.

Sales Employees
Sales promotion incentives are similar to those listed above and include com-mission related sales, competitions, token and points systems occurring over an extended period to encourage an on-going sales commitment by the sales force. Sales promotion is a marketing tool in its own right and should be planned, monitored and evaluated as such. It can be initiated either by the operation itself or by an external organization, and as with all other aspects of the marketing mix must be in line with the marketing objectives of the organization.

Personal Selling

Personal selling is a paid form of promoting a facility on a personal basis. One of the main characteristics of service industries is the in-creased contact time between service staff and customers, and the attitudes and behaviour of an operation's service employees are important parts of the total product the customer is buying. As with the other aspects of the promotion mix, advertising, public relations, merchandising and sales promotion, the objectives, requirements and techniques of personal selling need to be fully integrated into the overall marketing policy of the organization. Service employees are one of the most important assets of a catering operation. Too frequently waiters, bar staff, counter assistants, are seen only as 'order takers' and not as sales people. Particularly in large organizations, such as hotels, which have there own sales department, it is too easy for service staff to see themselves merely as servers of the facilities' foods and beverages. The fact that an establishment may have a sales department does not relieve the catering department of its sales functions and responsibilities.

When customers enter a restaurant there first personal contact with the restaurant staff is usually the waiter who shows them to their table. How often is that same customer presented with the menu and then left to ponder for a consider-able time without being asked if they would like a drink while considering the menu. A potential drink sale is lost immediately. When the waiter comes to take customers' orders there is another chance for the employee to promote the menu, perhaps the restaurant's specialty, a side salad, additional vegetables, wine to accompany the meal, rather than simply being an order taker. At the end of the meal the presentation of the dessert and liqueur trolleys can do much to revitalize a customer's palate, rather than the waiter merely asking if sweet or coffee are required.

Some establishments operate training programmes for service staff to help increase their awareness of the different ways in which they personally can contribute to an operation's sale. These training programmes can include basic sales functions of the waiter, such as asking customers if they would like a drink when they arrive at the restaurant to more in depth sensitivity training.

In catering spectrum, where there is a much longer contact time between service staff and customers, such as in haute cuisine or specialty restaurants, the 'personal touch' plays a more important role in the total service product. Also at this level, the technical knowledge of the service staff assumes greater importance.

Some operations encourage their staff to sell by providing incentives. If the waiter sold more food and beverages than the average for that restaurant incentives are paid. Investigating service staff in this way, however, needs to be introduced with sensitivity so that the wrong type of competitiveness between staff does not develop to the detriment of the restaurant.

Whatever the level of catering operation and the amount of sales training given, there is a need for service staff to become more alert to customers' needs by listening to and observing and identifying what their needs are for that particular meal; this information may then be quantified by management for possible future action.

The marketing of a catering operation must be effectively planned, organized and monitored throughout all its stages. The successes and failures of its promotional campaigns and those of its competitors should be studied and reviewed when possible. Good advertising, merchandising, public relations and sales promotion are difficult. They are areas of food and beverage management that often require considerable financial outlay, but which have no guarantee of success. Caterers are faced with a variety of promotional tools and techniques and whichever they choose, so will have others; they must compete there-fore not only with the other facilities' catering products but also with their marketing campaigns. Alone, advertising does not sell. It is there to stimulate interest, and to influence a customer towards buying an operation's product above those of its competitors. The customer's action is translated into a purchase at the point of sale, further stimulated by effective merchandising and possibly sales promotion techniques, all working together in a favorable environment created by good public relations.

Bibliography

Andrews, Sudhir, *Food and Beverage Service: Training Manual* 1982, Tata MCGraw Hill, New Delhi.

Buick, John W., Quality Control, *Hospitality* October, 1980.

Buttle, F., (1994), Marketing and merchandising, in Davis, B. and Lockwood, A. (eds.) *Food and Beverage Management; A Selection of Readings*, Butter worth-Heinemann: Oxford.

Buzzell, R.D. and Gale, B.T. (1987), *The PIMS Principles-linking Strategy to Performance*, New York, The Free Press.

Cassee, E. and Reuland, R.J. (1983), Hospitality in hospitals, in Rehuland, R.J. and Casee, E. (eds.), The *Management of Hospitality*, Oxford: Pergamon Press, pp. 143-63.

Charley, Helen, *Food Science*, Ed. 2, 1982, Jhon Wiley, New York.

Coltman, M. (1987), *Hospitality Management Accounting*, 3rd edn. New York: Van Nostrand Reinhold.

Crosby, P.B. (1982), *Quality Without Tears*, New York: McGraw Hill.

Deming, W.E. (1982), *Quality, Productivity and Competitive Position,* Massachusetts Institute of Technology, Center for Advanced Engineering Study: Massachusetts.

Dhingra, C.K. and Malik, R.K., *Modern Detergents and Soap Industries* (Small scale industries, Pub. No. 29) n.d. Small Indust─ Institute: Delhi.

Doswell, R. and Gamble, Paul R. (1979), *Hotels and Tourism Project*. Barrie & Je

Fitzgerad, L., Johnston, R. Brignall, S., Silvestro, R. and Voss, C. (1991), *Performance measurement in service business*. London: The Chartered Institute of Management Accountants.

Flood, R.L. (1993), *Beyond TQM*, Chichester: John Wiley and Sons.

Food Service in Institutions Ed. 5, 1977, Hohn Wiley, New York.

Gamble, P. Lockwood, A. and Messenger, S. (1994), *Management Skills in the European Hospitality Industry*, 48th Annual CHRIE Conference, Palm Springs, July 27-30.

Goldmann, Mary E., *Planning and Serving Your Meals*, Ed. 2, 1959, McGraw Hill, New York.

Green, E.F., *et al.* (1987), *Profitable Food and Beverage Management: Operations*, Jenks, Oklahoma: Williams Books.

Huelin, A. and Jones, P. (1990), Thinking about catering systems, *International Journal of Operations and Production Management*, 10, No. 8, 42-52.

Kahrl, William L. (1977), *Advanced Modern Food and Beverage Service*, Prentice Hall, New Jersey.

Kasavana, M. and Smith, D. (1982), *Menu Engineering*, Michigan: Hospitality Publications.

Kinder, Faye, Green, Nancy R., Harris, Nathalyn (1984), *Meal Management* 6th ed., MacMillan Publishing Co., New York.

Kinder, Faye (1973), *Meal Management*, Ed. 4, Macmillan; London.

Kotas, R. and Davis, B. (1980), *Food and Beverage Control*, Glasgow: Blackie.

Kotschevar, Lendal H. (1975), *Quantity Food Production*, Ed. 3, Cahners, Boston.

Levinson, C. (1976), *Food and Beverage Operation*, Prentice Hall, New Jersey.

Potter, Normal N. (1976), *Food Science*, Ed. 2, Avi Pub., Connecticut.

Terrel, Margaret E. (1971), *Professional Food Preparation*, Jonh Wiley, New York.

Watson, Olive B. (1968), *School and Institutional Lunchroom Management*, Parker, New York.

Index